MAKING 21ST CENTURY DISCIPLE MAKERS

Jonathan Cashman

Britney Cashman

Andrew Sargent PH.D.

ISBN: 1537435000
ISBN-13: 978-1537435008

DEDICATION

For Doug Joseph, thanks for kicking me in the seat of the pants to write this book. For David and Shelby Northup, and John and Mary Gunderson. Thank you for your tireless discipleship in those early years, and for putting up with all of my crazy passions to do great things for God. For my loving wife, and writing partner, I am truly a man most blessed. ~Jonathan

For Pastor Rick and Pam, the wonderful people of Faith Assembly and my teachers at First Assembly Christian Academy. Thank you for teaching me the Word of God, and for inspiring me and encouraging me to pursue the call of God on my life. For my amazing parents, brothers, and husband Jonathan – your love and support mean the world to me. ~Britney

For Charlie Brown, DMin. Your brief mentorship at a crucial time in my development meant more to me than you could possibly imagine. You were a beacon of hope. ~Andrew

TABLE OF CONTENTS

ACKNOWLEDGMENTS

We'd like to acknowledge Lee Steffen at Penguin Creative for lending us his amazingly creative eye, for the Cashmans picture and many other quality photos that came out of that shoot. To Jason Velazquez with Quezart for his cover design, thanks for keeping it simple, clean and awesome and for being super-responsive to every change, nudge and tweak. And what can we say about Nick Fogarty, who came through during a personally difficult and entangled weekend to do a photo shoot with Dr. Sargent. He looks half-human through your photographic magic.

INTRODUCTION

A scholar, a pastor and a worship leader walk into a bar… sounds like the opening of a good joke, but these are the perspectives from which this book is written—three different generations of people, from three different walks of life whose hearts are fixated on one thing… making disciple-makers.

Jonathan Cashman, a Prodigal Son, saved out of a life of sex, drugs and rock n' roll, walked immediately into a discipleship relationship, defining "Christian" for him going forward. He brings the perspective of a non-Christian outsider who experienced God in a radical way, but faced great challenges in the discipleship process. The lessons he learned as he developed from prodigal singer/songwriter, turned believer, to disciple, to disciple-maker, to worship and discipleship pastor, to travelling musical and discipleship evangelist bring an honest insight into the real struggles the Church faces today in its commission to GO and make disciples.

Britney Cashman, a Christian recording artist, worship leader, and women's small group organizer brings a millennial's perspective to disciple making in the 21st century. She was raised in both a Jewish and occasional church-attending household, and overcame the challenges of both a broken home as well as a (seemingly innocent at the time) spiritual elitist/end time fanatical/pseudo-Christian cult. She gleans from her past experiences to bring a poignant sociological insight into reaching today's younger generations. Together with her husband Jonathan, she is committed to spreading the gospel and helping churches make healthy disciple-making disciples for Christ.

Andrew Sargent, a quintessential church kid turned biblical scholar and professor, struggled long with his inability to elicit true discipleship from those around him. He brings the perspective of discipleship gone wrong from his experiences with the shepherding movement of the 80's. While having many fine teachers through the long journey from College freshman to Ph.D., he found few who showed an inclination to guide him with the heart of a father on the path of THE Father. Armed with a determination to be the mentor he always felt denied, he has dedicated himself to taking his teaching beyond the classroom into the lives of students, developing and discipling Christian leaders worldwide.

Jesus' famous last words to His Church before he exited the earth were, "Go and make disciples of all the nations… teaching them to observe all things that I have commanded you" (Matt 28:19). This is what we consider to be the Great Commission; as a disciple of Jesus, it is *your* mission, should you choose to accept it. For many, however, the Great Commission has become the Great Omission. GO is designed to help you fulfill the call on your life as a disciple of Jesus Christ to GO and make disciples. We hope our combined perspectives and experiences will become a motivator and a compass in your own journey as a commissioned disciple-maker.

1

COME THEY

Matthew 28:18-20

*All authority has been given to Me in heaven and on earth.
Go therefore and make disciples of all the nations, baptizing them in
the name of the Father and of the Son and of the Holy Spirit,
teaching them to observe all things that I have commanded you*

Jonathan:

"She's going to leave me!" Keith was in agony, his voice faltered on the line as he tried to restrain himself from crying.

It was Tuesday, and I was the pastor on call, which meant that I'd be answering the phone at church if anyone needed to speak with a pastor. I was a complete stranger to Keith and him to me, but as I listened to him pour out his heart over the phone, I knew I'd have to do more than pray for him and go about my day.

"See, I gave my life to Christ a few days ago and realized that I needed to confess some things to my wife… some things that I'd been doing," he said. There was a pause on the line, then he continued. "I've been sleeping with prostitutes… and I've been watching a lot of porn and I knew God wanted me to confess to my wife, and so I did, last night, and now she wants to leave me." He paused again, caught his breath, then uttered, "I have a two year old son! She's going to leave me!" Sobs poured through the line

I felt bad for him, but what could I do? Was praying enough? What kind of advice could I give? *You might want to start packing dude...* I don't remember learning how to handle a situation like this in any of my classes in Bible College. I could invite him to church? That would both sate my conscience and get me off the phone, and who knows, maybe that's all I needed to do. Regular church attendance might help over time, but suggesting it wasn't enough to meet his immediate crisis. This guy needed big-time help. He needed spiritual guidance and direction.

Not that I doubt the power of prayer, but any prayer I might have prayed there on the phone could have seemed shallow, almost like I was brushing him off, *Lord, please don't let this guy's wife leave him for sleeping with prostitutes, amen... Okay Buddy, I've got to go, now.*

I'd just started a new small group at a Starbucks near my house, on the outskirts of Orlando. We were meeting that very night, so I said, "Listen, I meet on Tuesdays at Starbucks in Longwood, why don't you come out tonight?" He agreed; I prayed; we hung up. I wondered the rest of that day if he'd really show. To my amazement, he did, looking like a man who'd just stepped out of a war. My first success was getting him to blink.

To put it lightly, Keith was a mess. He couldn't hold a conversation, had a hard time listening, would talk and talk and then say, "What was I talking about?" We weren't sure ourselves. He was confused, heartbroken, scared and self-medicating. As I pieced together his story, I could hear his heart for the Lord... he'd risked life as he knew it on a confession he felt God wanted him to make. He also wanted to believe that God would turn things around in his marriage, if he stayed true to Him, but had to confront the unimagined possibility that he may have gained God and lost all else in the process. He wanted to hope, but he was frightened.

That night marked a turning point for Keith; he'd made real friends, he was listened to, prayed for, cared for and, at the end, left our group smiling. I told Keith that I would commit myself to helping him, to mentor him in his spiritual walk. We developed a plan for him to pray for and care for his wife and, most of all, a plan for developing a patient trust in God for the outcome, whatever it might be. It wasn't going to be easy.

Keith called me a lot in the days and weeks to come. He even rang in the middle of a late night Christmas Eve service. My wife saw his name pop up on caller-ID, and nodded resignedly, knowing I had to take it.

"She's going to leave me!" Keith cried when I answered.

Then Keith's wife called. "I'm going to leave him!"

It was rough going for a while. Keith showed up every Tuesday at Starbucks, and we, as a group, would teach him, care for him, listen to him and pray for him. Week by week, I began to see a change in Keith as he grew in his relationship with Christ.

Eventually, as hurt, skeptical, and reluctant to risk further on Keith as she'd been, his wife saw a change in him, as well. As one can imagine, it wasn't easy for her, but, after about a year, she believed that the Lord had done a genuine work in Keith, recommitted to the relationship, and committed her life to Christ, as well.

Keith now leads a small group of his own and is mentoring and helping to disciple other guys just like himself.

There are Keiths everywhere. They are the ones that are hurting, issue laden, needy. Keiths love the Lord, but desperately need one thing—personal discipleship.

OUR MISSION:

Jesus' famous last words before he ascended began with the great verb—GO! It is His great commission to His Church, their mission statement. It is thus, your mission, to GO. GO, and make disciples. GO into all the world and make disciples. GO and make disciples, teaching them to obey all the things that Christ as commanded. (Matthew 28:19-20)

In the King James Version of the Bible, Jesus says, "GO ye." In our practice of church, however, we tend more toward a "Come they" mentality. When we associate ministry and outreach with services, buildings, programs, and pastors, we imagine that our highest responsibility to the lost is to get them into church.

We can all fall victim to this "come they" mentality. Even with Keith, I didn't "GO" to him; he called me. Once he reached out, it was easy to follow up. The "GOING" came after, when God sent me into his life to be there for him, to pray with him, to be a friend, a council. Keith was in need of discipleship; he reached out to those who might help, and stumbled upon me. But what of the ones who are in need around us who don't reach out? They're everywhere. Are you going to them? Are we?

WHAT IS A DISCIPLE?

Upwards of 80% of Americans self-identify as Christian. The word Christian, however, was never used by Jesus to define his followers. The word Christian was originally and insult, a by-word conjured by the enemies of the church—"little Christs," they'd jeer. Jesus used a more demanding terms. He called them Disciples, which in Greek requires binding one's self to another to learn all that such a one can teach, and in English roots itself in that more horrible of ideas—discipline.

We can define a *disciple* as one who is disciplined in conforming into the image and teaching of Jesus. A disciple is one who follows Jesus' commands and, therefore, follows His final earthly command to make disciples, teaching others to do the same.

WHO ARE YOUR DISCIPLES?

These days, my wife and I travel fulltime with our ministry, leading worship and speaking at a different church every Sunday. At each visit, I teach on the importance of fulfilling the Great Commission and ask the congregation this question— "Who are your disciples?" Some time ago, the Lord put on my heart that there ought to always be people in my life that I could point to and say, they are my disciples, these are the people I have mentored, or are mentoring. Jesus prayed for and chose His disciples and in the same way I believe that God sends people to us, places people in our lives, on our hearts, to mentor, teach and, well… disciple.

The Lord said that "The harvest is great, but the laborers are few." Apparently, there isn't much of a harvest problem, but, rather, a laborer problem. Therefore, if we want a great harvest (and don't we?) then we need to pray for and raise up laborers. The greatest way to raise up laborers is to make disciples. I can see no other way.

So… how are you doing with this? Who are your disciples?

ARE WE DOING IT RIGHT?

"You're the next generation of the Church," our 60-something Bible College professor announced to our 20-something class, then asked, "Are we doing it right?"

Let me ask you. Are we? It's a huge question.

Perhaps, we should step back a second and reconsider the

nature of it.

What does "right" mean? What does success look like for the church?

Can we really say that there is a one size fits all answer to this question? We have to qualify the "win." We need to define our goals. We need to evaluate and reevaluate how effective our methods are in achieving those goals.

If Jesus' commission to the church—GO into all the world and make disciples, teaching them to obey everything he's commanded—is our purpose, then we need to ask, need to constantly ask, how are we doing with this? How are you, as a part of the Church, doing with this? Who are your disciples? Can you think of specific people whom you mentor spiritually?

How is your church doing with this? Are you part of a disciple-making organism?

I don't ask this like some crazed and annoyed know-it-all prophet of doom kicking in the back door of the sanctuary during morning worship to accuse with gnarled pointed finger, but as one who is in ministry, asking this question in the mirror often—Am I doing it right? Let's take an honest look at then. Let's find out?.

2

 WHERE ARE WE GOING?

JOHN 4:35

Behold, I say to you, lift up your eyes and look at the fields, for they are already white for harvest!

When we turn to consider the success or failure of the church, the tendency is to allow personal bias to interpret the data. If I feel the church is an utter failure, I can find the stats to back that up. If I am blown away at the efficiency of and effectiveness of Church in the world, I can find the stats to back that up as well. To find an honest perspective, a true and real look at the landscape of the Church as it relates to it's effectiveness in fulfilling the Great Commission, two things are needed—Properly gathered and critically evaluated statistics and appropriate expectations.

When we studied the raw data on the Church in America (based on the disciple-making criteria), and crossed referenced that with our combined decades of diverse personal experiences and with the stories of the many we've met over the years, we realized that whatever strengths the church has and has had over the centuries (which are many and significant for the world), disciple-making does not appear to be one of them today.

A bald consideration of the numbers and of the testimonies behind those numbers is scandalous. But, let's start out by stating that we believe in the Church, want to edify the Church, hope for and pray for the ongoing success of the Church. No institution in the history of the world has done more good for the human race than the Church. It is and has been a vital force for divine guidance and benefit to man since its founding. Christ is the hope of the world manifest through His body the Church. This book is not a "let's dog the church book," but rather, it is written to help those in the Church become more effective in their outreach and more efficient in their discipleship. The Western World is experiencing a major cultural shift, and we, the Church need to the address and respond to the tensions that are rapidly growing in our society. We have relational breakdowns and need to build better bridges to reach those on the other side of the divide, if we hope to convey our message effectively.

Criticism is the laziest of all disciplines. We are interested in resolution not complaints. It is easy to see the imperfections in the Church and to let our hearts cry, "Tear it down!" or "I'm outa here!" We, however, are interested in helping to make the imperfect Church a little less imperfect, a little more effective, because the Church is Christ's instrument in the world; we love the Church, warts and all, just as Jesus does.

Unfortunately, part of process improvement is looking at the warts straight on. It would be ineffective for us to propose solutions to problems that you don't see. When we perceive the illness we will seek a cure.

According to Barna Group Research 49% of Americans claim to be actively churched, claim to attend a Christian church regularly. While this is a positive when compared to nations with a low single digit church attendance, for America, this represents a loss of nearly 25 million church attenders in the last 7 years alone. Churchlessness is on the rise in America.

The rise of churchlessness in America

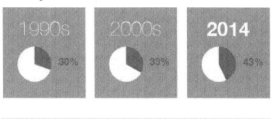

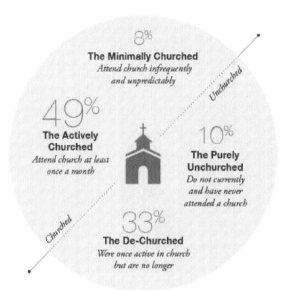

People are leaving or staying away; they are either *de-churched* or *un-churched*. Presently, over 162 million people in America have little to nothing to do with the Christian church. This chapter aims to help us take a good honest look at who these people are and the reasons for their aversion to church. Our hope is that in uncovering these issues that your heart will cry out to participate in a resolution.

THE DE-CHURCHED

Barna Group identifies a huge portion of the American population as *De-churched*, those who were once regular church attenders who no longer attend. These account for a whopping 33% of the American population… that is over 100 million people. 1000 might be considered a fluke, 10,000 an interesting pattern, a million a movement, but 100 million is an epidemic. If we include the minimally churched, those who rarely attend, we can add another 8% to this, or, in practical terms, over 125 million people in total.

Bottom line… we have a problem with people leaving the church.

It would be easy to brush these numbers off, to consider these De-Churched people to be the curmudgeons, the whiners, those that didn't get their way, or the stubborn and rebellious, the hard hearted who were unwilling to listen to leadership, or just wanted to live immoral lives without criticism. This would be a mistake. Not only would this be a hasty generalization of a complex group, this portrayal doesn't line up with the data. While the implacable may make up a portion of these folks, according to recent research, it is actually a smaller portion than you may imagine. The majority of those in this epidemic have been the active, the educated, the involved; they represent a demographic of Christians who served in churches, or held positions of leadership, even on staff. These were the movers and the shakers. They have left their churches, but not their faith.

Josh Packard, Ph.D and Ashleigh Hope have done extensive study of this De-Churched group and released their findings in the book, *Church Refugees*. They've chosen the term *refugees* carefully to describe a serious portion of the De-Churched, saying,

Refugees are people who've been forced from their homes—where they'd prefer to stay—for fear of persecution. That, in a nutshell, describes the De-Churched. They feel they've been forced to leave a place they consider home because they feel a kind of spiritual persecution and it would be dangerous, spiritually, for them to remain. They tell stories of frustration, humiliation, judgment, embarrassment, and fear that caused them to leave the church. They remark time and again that they worked diligently for reform within the church but felt the church was exclusively focused on its own survival and resistant to change. If they stayed, they would risk further estrangement from their spiritual selves, from God, and from a religion they still believe in."

"They're the ones who, prior to leaving, showed up at worship every week and tithed. …They have the greatest social and political power. And when they leave, they take all of that with them. …Our interviews indicate that the De-Churched are among the most dedicated people in any congregation. …They display an extreme level of dedication and devotion to God and religion, and they earnestly believe that the institutional church can be fixed and reclaimed. …They believe it's worth fighting for right up to the point where they don't."[i]

These are the disenfranchised sheep, forced from their pens to wander the hills untended. If the Church is meant to be an extension of the work of the Good Shepherd, but forsakes the heart of the Good Shepherd under bureaucratic pressure to preserve the institution, it has become self-defeating. Such a shift always comes at the cost of the welfare of the sheep. If shepherds become more concerned with the appeal and efficiency of the sheep pen than they do the health and vitality of the sheep in the pen, they've lost their way; they've forgotten their primary purpose as shepherds. Do we GO to these people? Do we wander the wilderness seeking them out? No. According to statistics, rather than *going* to seek out these disenfranchised sheep, we are the ones who allowed them to wander off in a hundred different ways.

THERE IS THE DOOR:
CRITICISM—THE UNPARDONABLE SIN

"If you don't like it, there's the door!" Have you heard this before? It comes in many flavors. Sometimes it's coated with sugary spiritual sprinkles with words like, unity, seasons, harmony, mission, vision, sometimes with spiritual arsenic, loaded with terms like rebellion, "in sin", spirit of Jezebel. It would seem that to many leaders, the true unpardonable sin is criticism. For these, there is no desire to understand, or listen, no interest in reconciling disagreements. It is easier to walk with yes men than to wade through messy intimacy and honest accountability that come naturally with the familial bond of community.

We've experienced this ourselves more times and, sadly, in more churches than we care to recount; we hear similar stories in our travels. Recently, we had dinner with a small community of people that would fall into this Church Refugee category. Here are the characters; we had an Elder, a worship pastor, a youth pastor, a deacon, a graphic designer/small group leader, and several members of the worship team. They were founding or long-term members of a large, thriving, highly relational and steadily growing church. The founding pastor built the church around interpersonal communication, mutual respect, and worked cooperatively in both the setting and accomplishing of the church's goals.

A few years ago, this pastor felt called to other pastures and left the church in the hands of a well trained Elder and Deacon board who continued the work successfully while they sought out a new pastor. When they found their man, one who professed great respect for their Elder led model (not elder run model—they were adamant on the distinction), they welcomed him joyfully.

What followed, however, was a rapid and steady breaking of relationships in favor of email communication, dictatorial demands without the possibility of discussion, and incremental takeover and micromanagement of every facet of church life, systematic isolation of the familial bonds of the leaders, dismissive "unbalanced hierarchy" between the deacons & elders & pastor… In their words, he put "policy over people."

In short, the culture shifted. They went from being a relational, Elder-led church, to a policy driven Pastor-run church. When some of these leaders at our dinner table questioned and challenged certain changes and policies, when they contested the heart of how policies were being delivered, a conflict of ideals arose. Without conferring together, each at our dinner party felt that they had been separated from the true heart of their calling. Each felt culpable for their part in allowing the personal, shepherding, discipling spirit to bleed away. Each unaware of the actions of the others, sought to sound the alarm with the pastor personally. His response in a nutshell—"You don't like it, there's the door."

After conceding that there would be no resolution to the conflict, a key Elder stepped down quietly. This degraded the situation rapidly. Rather than seeking restoration with him, rather than going to him, the pastor went into damage control mode. He went to anyone he feared might side with the elder, implying that they needed to make a choice—they were with him or against him… and there's the door.

One by one, they chose the door.

This wasn't a church split; they did not confer together in secret, planning some childish escape. They did, however, gather together slowly over the following months to sate their desire for community without recommitting to a Church. For this, for their gathering together, they are demonized by the surrounding Christian community, ridiculed privately and publicly and told to repent or face stronger persecution and public ostracization.

Poor conflict resolution, usually based on a radical misperception of what familial Christian community ought to be, always comes with a human cost.

We would like to point out something about these folks that agrees with Packard's interpretation of the De-churched—they are not angry. They express frustration with a broken system that is geared towards its own survival, a system that in their minds isn't working, a system focused on building an efficient organization rather than building community. Though they may have reason to be, these folks are not jaded. They weren't frustrated with structure, but with the prohibition and general stifling of creativity and community within that structure.

This is something that demands our attention—when we are too focused on the work of the Lord that we forget the Lord of the work, or the people invested in the work, we all lose.

WHY PEOPLE LEAVE THE CHURCH

According to Packard and Hope's research, there are two main reasons why people leave their church—*Judgment,* both implicit and explicit, and *Bureaucracy.*

According to the research, *implicit judgment* is the most

pervasive. Implicit judgment is "felt or perceived rather than overtly expressed." It, "…typically occurred between congregants and included dirty looks, ostracism, jealousy, whispering, and rumors." Packard notes, "These kinds of behaviors can be found in any social group, but they can be particularly damaging when they happen in church."[ii]

Explicit judgment is direct, openly expressed derision. It comes with an air of pride and a pointed finger. Packard and Hope state, "Our respondents uniformly expressed comfort with the idea of God as a judge (though they had very different ideas about what this would look like), but they were also unanimously opposed to people acting in this capacity.

A feeling of judgment, in any social sphere, comes with dire consequences for a group. People who feel judged generally become defensive and withdraw from a group, but usually only after a period of gradual disengagement and resistance."[iii] It is true that unchecked judgment can become the greatest destroyer of relationships and community.

Bureaucracy becomes a byword in church when policies, procedures and programs trump people. According to the research, people are "walking away because they're convinced that the structures and *bureaucracy* of the church are inhibiting their ability to serve God. They see the church as oriented only to its own survival. Instead of empowering, they find the church to be stifling. Over time, they've become convinced that their efforts and energies could be better spent serving God outside of the church."[iv]

Hopefully by now we can see how these issues are counterintuitive to the Great Commission, to "GO make disciples." Jesus gave this commission to His Church and comes to us both individually (you and I) and collectively (as His Church) to "GO!" But how can we GO together if we can't even *stand* together? What are we "Going" with? What does our message to the world look like if we are so splintered? How can we GO if we don't love one another? What's our purpose become if not to GO make disciples? We will uncover more on this later.

THE UN-CHURCHED

If I were trying to reach a tribe in Paupa New Guinea that had never heard of Jesus, or Christianity, what would I need to do in order to effectively communicate the gospel to them? In addition to understanding the gospel, Scripture and theology, I would need to understand them, their language, their culture, their perceptions of me and my message.

In many ways, a similar approach is necessary when trying to reach the Un-Churched in America.

Many of us are so accustomed to the culture of the Church that we have lost any sense of how we are perceived by those outside the church. We are a foreign culture to the unchurched. They don't understand our beliefs, our language, or our standards. Being foreign to them, they often can't hear our hearts through our strange rhetoric and behavior, and our promotion of a lifestyle that is utterly alien to them. They can't even imagine that such a life is possible. Our "hypocrisy" tells them its not.

In their book, *UnChristian*, David Kinnaman and Gabe Lyons from Barna Research studied thousands of 'outsiders' impressions of Christians and while we may comfort ourselves in our ability to argue them down, it would be foolish, from a missionary perspective, to overlook them.

In their exploration, they found that, "One crucial insight kept popping up. In studying thousands of outsiders' impressions, it is clear that Christians are primarily perceived for what they stand against. We have become famous for what we oppose, rather than who we are for... Outsiders believe Christians do not like them because of what they do, how they look, or what they believe. They feel minimized—or worse, demonized—by those who love Jesus.

These issues may get your blood pumping, but they are important issues because often they reflect very real ways in which the Christian community has mistakenly portrayed itself to a skeptical generation… The most common 6 points of skepticism and objections raised by outsiders are as follows:

1. *Hypocritical.* Outsiders consider us hypocritical—saying one thing and doing another—and they are skeptical of our morally superior attitudes. They say Christians pretend to be something unreal, conveying a polished image that is not accurate. Christians think the church is only a place for virtuous and morally pure people.

2. *Too focused on getting converts.* Outsiders wonder if we genuinely care about them. They feel like targets rather than people. They question our motives when we try to help them "get saved," despite the fact that many of them have already "tried" Jesus and experienced church before.

3. *Antihomosexual.* Outsiders say that Christians are bigoted and show disdain for gays and lesbians. They say Christians are fixated on curing homosexuals and on leveraging political solutions against them.

4. *Sheltered.* "Christians are thought of as old-fashioned, boring, and out of touch with reality. Outsiders say we do not respond to reality in appropriately complex ways, preferring simplistic solutions and answers. We are not willing to deal with the grit and grime of people's lives.

5. *Too political.* Another common perception of Christians is that we are overly motivated by a political agenda, that we promote and represent politically conservative interests and issues. Conservative Christians are often thought of as right-wingers.

6. *Judgmental.* Outsiders think of Christians as quick to judge others. They say we are not honest about our attitudes and perspectives about other people. They doubt that we really love people as we say we do." [v]

The fact that the un-churched have these perceptions does not make the un-churched right about their expectations; it does not even make them right about us, though they are, no doubt right about some of us. It does not require us to change our theology and moral convictions in order to win and disciple them. What it does demand, however, is some deep awareness of the things that stand as barriers between our message and their ears. We need self-awareness in the work. We don't need to be less theological or hold lower moral standards, but we do need to be more relational.

CONCLUSION

Both the De-Churched and the Un-Churched are our mission field. They are those who Christ has called and commissioned us to GO *to*—to disciple, to reach, to love. It is apparent that we have a lot of work to do. It can seem an insurmountable task.

Jesus said, "The harvest is plentiful, but the *laborers* are few. Therefore pray earnestly to the Lord of the harvest to send out *laborers* into his harvest." (Luke 10:2)

There isn't a harvest problem, but a laborer problem. How do we raise up laborers? Pray for them and make disciples. Let's keep in mind how Jesus did it. Jesus spent 3 years with 12 guys and changed the world. He had a heart for people and saw people as His purpose. He called them, committed to them, taught them, led them, empowered them and sent them to GO into the harvest to make other disciple-making disciples.

[i] Josh Packard Ph.D. & Ashleigh Hope, Church Refugees, Loveland: Group Publishing (2015), P.21-36

[ii] Josh Packard Ph.D. & Ashleigh Hope, Church Refugees, Loveland: Group Publishing (2015), P.21-36

iii Josh Packard Ph.D. & Ashleigh Hope, Church Refugees, Loveland: Group Publishing (2015), P.21-36

iv Josh Packard Ph.D. & Ashleigh Hope, Church Refugees, Loveland: Group Publishing (2015), P.21-36

v David Kinnaman and Gabe Lyons, UnChristian, Grand Rapids: Baker Books (2007), P.31-32

3

 HEART OF THE FATHER

Luke 15:1-3

Then all the tax collectors and the sinners drew near to Him to hear Him. And the Pharisees and scribes complained, saying, "This Man receives sinners and eats with them." So He spoke...

"The Son of Man has come to seek and to save that which was lost" (Luke 19:10). This was Jesus' personal mission statement. In this way, Jesus exemplified the heart of the Father. His goal was seeking and saving, finding and making disciples, but this was not always widely understood, or received. In fact, Jesus had the hardest time getting those who allegedly knew the Word of God to understand and reflect the heart of God—a father's heart.

During His earthly ministry, Jesus was repeatedly coming into contact with sinners and saints, bad guys and the supposed-to-be good guys. The ruling religious class of Pharisees, Sadducees, Priests and Scribes, those who knew the Word of God, were constantly at odds with Jesus for His *receiving* and *eating* with "sinners," even repentant sinners.

During one of these particular moments, while Jesus was catching flack for His choice of dinner guests, He decided, in typical Jesus fashion, to teach a valuable spiritual lesson. Using three parables that express the heart of the father toward His creatures—*The Lost Sheep, The Lost Coin & The Lost Son*—Jesus turned the tables on their question. What needs explaining, in light of God's heart for His children, is *not* why Jesus choses to eat with tax gatherers and sinners, but, rather, why these religious leaders don't.

These three parables could come under the heading, "God Wants to Party." In the first parable, He explains that if a man were to have 100 sheep and lose one, he'd naturally leave the 99 to search for the one and finding it, he'd return home, call his friends and have a party. Likewise, there is joy in heaven over one sinner who repents. The second parable is like the first. He describes the heart of God in seeking the lost as a woman who loses a sentimentally precious coin and upon a diligent search of her house, finds it, calls her friends and neighbors and has a party. Then Jesus tells them the Parable of The Lost Son, or what is commonly called, The Prodigal Son. Here, a son is lost, returns, and his father throws a party.

The Prodigal Son is one of the greatest and most popular parables Jesus ever told. The gospel is there; you and I are there; human failure and repentance are there; the heart of God is there, displayed for all the sinners and saints to see. As such, it sets the stage for our discussion on the great commission. This can't be underscored enough. We can't undertake biblical disciple-making until we have the heart of the Father for His children… *all* His children.

There are two sons in this parable. Each represents one of the groups in Jesus' audience. Then we have the father in the story dealing with each of his sons differently. So let's take this parable in two stages, the heart of the Father as it relates to the younger son and the heart of the Father as it relates to the older son. We'll start with the younger son.

THE PRODIGAL SON

He said: "A certain man had two sons. And the younger of them said to his father, 'Father, give me the portion of goods that falls to me.' So he divided to them his livelihood. And not many days after, the younger son gathered all together, journeyed to a far country, and there wasted his possessions with prodigal living. But when he had spent all, there arose a severe famine in that land, and he began to be in want. Then he went and joined himself to a citizen of that country, and he sent him into his fields to feed swine. And he would gladly have filled his stomach with the pods that the swine ate, and no one gave him anything.

"But when he came to himself, he said, 'How many of my father's hired servants have bread enough and to spare, and I perish with hunger! I will arise and go to my father, and will say to him, "Father, I have sinned against heaven and before you, and I am no longer worthy to be called your son. Make me like one of your hired servants."'

"And he arose and came to his father. But when he was still a great way off, his father saw him and had compassion, and ran and fell on his neck and kissed him. And the son said to him, 'Father, I have sinned against heaven and in your sight, and am no longer worthy to be called your son.'

"But the father said to his servants, 'Bring out the best robe and put it on him, and put a ring on his hand and sandals on his feet. And bring the fatted calf here and kill it, and let us eat and be merry; for this my son was dead and is alive again; he was lost and is found.' And they began to be merry. (Luke 15:11-24 *NKJV*)

Jonathan:

The younger son left his father to pursue a prodigal life, a wasteful life. So there he is, out at the clubs every night; he buys a fancy pad, a sporty new car… but then a famine comes. He doesn't exactly have a sound financial plan, so, he goes broke.

Problems get worse when he can't find work, and the only work he can find is feeding pigs. This is not exactly the ideal occupation for a good Jewish boy, but with this analogy, Jesus makes His point. He is portraying the moral and physical degradation of a wasteful and sinful lifestyle. It says, he gladly would have dined on pig food, but, "no one gave him anything." You know things are pretty bad, when you're so hungry that you've got a hankering for pig slop, but still can't get any.

It is important for us to understand where this younger son is coming from in order for us to relate to those who have come out of a similar, wasteful lifestyle, who have to deal with the effects of their past prodigal mentalities.

Personally, I relate to this guy and to this part of the parable, probably more than most, because this was me. I know the feeling of leaving your father's house to pursue a life of wastefulness; I know that famine; I know that pigsty; I know that feeling of wanting the proverbial pig slop and not being able to get it.

When I was 13, I pestered my dad into buying me an electric guitar. I watched the movie, *Back to the Future*, and seeing Marty McFly ripping through "Johnny Be Goode" on a red Gibson 350 did me in. My father finally buckled under the pressure and bought me a black Fender Stratocaster guitar and a small amp. I locked myself away in my room, learning my guitar lessons, the scales and songs, only coming out for the occasional meal and shower. Soon, I met some other guys who played guitar and were in real rock bands. They smoked, swore, drank beer and even had sex (so we heard). They wore dark clothes, had long hair and listened to heavy music. I wanted to be like them and started identifying myself with this musical culture.

So, at the ripe old age of 13, I started drinking beer and smoking. One night a friend of mine and I got a guy from the neighborhood to buy us a six pack of beer and we split it behind St. Mary's Church in Providence, RI. My father lived on the third floor of a three-tenement house in the inner city. I think it was built shortly after the pilgrims' landing; the stairs creaked too loudly for even a mouse to sneak in successfully. I had stashed a change of clothes on the second floor and some mouthwash to conceal my stank, but I *creaked, creaked, creaked* up the first flight of stairs, changed my clothes, rinsed my alcoholic beer mouth with alcoholic Listerine and came out to find my dad standing on the landing... a burly, shirtless, hairy, Italian father staring at me... or through me... peering into my very soul.

"What are you doing?" he asked. "Why are you sneaking into the house?"

I blanked. *Second floor? Second floor? Second floor? Oooo I know...* We had our washer and dryer on the second floor, so I rambled off something about checking the lint in the dryer. "You know, Dad, there are a lot of house fires these days... and... uhh... you can never be too careful..."

"Let me smell your breath," he said.

I was busted. He scolded me, then dragged me down the street and scolded my drinking buddy; his alcoholic parents certainly weren't going to scold him. Humiliated and irritated, I thought, *well if I want to live like this... I can't stay here.* I made a plan, packed my things and ran away from my father's house. Not to the streets mind you, but to Mom's, 20 minutes away. What a rebel! I felt I could get away with more at my mom's house. For the next ten years, to the chagrin of both of my parents, I lived my life as a prodigal, wasteful son.

HE CAME TO HIMSELF

Something happens to this young prodigal son in Jesus' story that changes his life. One day while sitting hungry in the pigsty, eagerly yearning to fill his stomach with a share of slop, he has a revelation. Jesus says that he "came to himself"—a changed heart summed up in one phrase. What was this great revelation? It was a revelation of both himself and of his father. He remembered his father. He realized that even his father's servants were in a better place than he was.

Could he just go home? Would he be received after squandering his inheritance? He knew he deserved to be rejected, but he devises a plan; he prepares a speech. "Father, I have sinned against heaven and before you, and I am no longer worthy to be called your son. Make me like one of your hired servants." *Ooo, yeah, that's good.* So he starts out on his reluctant and shame-filled journey home, his rehearsed speech ready on his lips.

This is the heart of many who sense their distance from God. Can they just come to God? There is that all-important moment in the sinner's heart that says, "I am no longer worthy to be called your child." It asks, "How could I be accepted after all I've done?" It often tries to find means of penance, ways to make it up, ways to counterbalance, to bridge the gap. It grovels like the Prodigal Son, "Make me like one of your hired servants."

Jesus, however, says that when the Prodigal's father saw him, he "had *compassion*, and ran and fell on his neck and kissed him." The son, obviously surprised by this acceptance, pulls out his speech. *Ahem...*"Father, I have sinned against heaven and in your sight and am no longer worthy to be called your son." It would seem that his father either ignored, or hardly noticed his son's speech, because, rather than responding to it, his father orders his servants to bring gifts of empowerment and inheritance—a robe to cover his shame, a ring to reestablish his role in the family, shoes to cover his feet, canceling his would-be slavery, a feast to strengthen and celebrate him. The son was received home with love... and a party.

Understanding the Father's heart for His wayward children can help us have compassion, grace and patience when it comes both to presenting the gospel and to the long arduous process of making disciples out of them. Those whose personal lives are rife with the consequences of all they've done and are doing by long ingrained habit are loved by the Father. God is eager to forgive, but many prodigals have a sense of trepidation about church, about coming to God, about identifying themselves as true sons and daughters of God in light of the lives they've lived. I can relate, but also know that it was my overwhelming sense of the Father's compassion, His unconditional love and acceptance, regardless of the life I'd been living, that overcame these fears. It was my friends' ongoing demonstration of this compassionate and loving heart of the Father that kept me strong when failure seemed a certainty.

SONS AND SERVANTS

I was 23, living out my rock n' roll dream with my band, The Trees, when my guitarist came to Christ and ruined all of our hopes of becoming rich and famous. Our band had been together since High School, and things were finally shaping up for us. We were proud of our music and had just signed to a small label, Big Noise Records. They were releasing our first album and about to showcase us to some major labels from New York when I got a call from Dave, our guitarist.

"I gave my life to Jesus Christ," he said. Those were his words, but I had no earthly idea what they meant. I had no context for them. I was brought up Catholic and had a modicum of God-belief, but it was nothing more than a mental assent to the fact that there was a God out there, somewhere. "Gave my life to Jesus Christ" made about as much sense to me as my barking dog. Dave then proceeded to give me an ultimatum. "If I'm going to stay in this band, then we need to do two Christian songs." Again, zero context, zero understanding… *what are "Christian songs?"*

I hesitantly agreed, probably more on the basis of curiosity and a desire to keep the band together than anything else. Dave came to our next band rehearsal with his wife, Shelby, and a small tape deck (an archaic machine once used by American youth to play music). At the end of practice, he announced that it was now time for us to learn our new Christian songs. They were the most hokey bluegrass tunes that we had ever heard.

My introduction to Christian music was a song he played from his tape deck called, "The Christian Life." The lyrics went like this: "My buddies left me when I came to Jesus. They say I'm missing a whole world of fun. I live without them and walk in the light… I liiiiiike the Chriii-istian life." *Why would you like that!? …Fast forward…* the next song wasn't much better; it was called, "I am a Pilgrim," and had lyrics like… well… "pilgrim," "yonder," "wearisome," "hem of His garment." We got Dave's ultimatum down from having to learn two "Christian songs," to just one. So, we reluctantly learned and rocked up, "I am a Pilgrim."

When rehearsal was over, a conversation started between Dave, Shelby and the guys in the band. Dave began to tell us about how God had changed his heart. He explained the gospel to us, talked about sin and the call of God. There was something different about my friend. One day he was just your average Dave and then, this guy… this caring, seemingly compassionate guy, who, knowing full well what he'd be in for by bringing Jesus to our rehearsal, took time to try to help us.

As I stated before, I had a small degree of belief in the existence of God, so I felt that I needed to let my friends off the hook, to let them know that they didn't need to preach to me. I was kind of on their side. I told them, "I believe in God." The words hung in the air like a lead cloud. As soon as I spoke them, I wished I hadn't.

Shelby turned to me and said, "Where's the fruit of that?"

Fruit? A little Christianeeze perhaps, but somehow, I got it—nothing in my life validated those words. They knew it. I knew it. My band knew it. I lived a particularly sinful lifestyle, and, because of this, I was kind of a jerk, selfish, and arrogant. I was battling with depression and had been self-medicating with drugs and alcohol to drown out the inner cry of my heart for love… for acceptance. Shelby's question got me thinking… a lot.

Over the next week or so my conversations with Dave and Shelby continued. We debuted "I am a Pilgrim," at the Blackstone Bar and Grille one Saturday night, and came back to my place and partied. The next morning, I was hungover, but woke early because I'd told Dave I would go to church with him. The curiosity was getting to me; I wanted experience God for myself, to know more about his church, his Christianity, about what had changed Dave.

Dave picked me up that morning and brought me to a typical, small, white, steepled New England church. As we walked in the back of the sanctuary, someone smiled big at me, called me Brother, stuck out his hand for me to shake, then handed me a bulletin. This church was a weeeeeee different from the Catholic churches I'd attended as a kid. There was a rock-ish band up front; people were raising their hands, singing fervently, yelling feverishly. I stood wide-eyed, not a little stunned in those foreign surroundings. The music was louder than I was expecting, but to my snobby musical sensibilities, it was terrible… No, seriously, the band was terrible and they sang their terrible songs to God. All the songs were alien to my ears, but as the people worshiped through this terrible music, something started to happen to me. I began to sense the loving presence of God and started to cry.

I slunk down in my chair, shoved my head in my arm and soaked my sleeve with tears. "Stop crying!" I remember saying over and over to myself, but I couldn't. It was if the Lord was taking a big scrub brush to my filthy sinful heart. I could sense Him, His Spirit, His love—it was all too much. I felt accepted by Him, but I struggled. Coming home, I struggled with every returning prodigal's question—*How can I be accepted after all I've done?*

I had the impression that the Lord was speaking to me, saying, "You'll write songs for *Me* now." This was a problem. Because, well… I didn't like bluegrass music and the sort of stuff I was hearing in that church wasn't much better—my entire Christian Music experience to date. I sat through the rest of the service as one struck by lightning: numb, confused and not a little bit amazed.

Dave, Shelby and I returned to my house, lousy with debris and passed out partiers from the night before. I gave everyone the boot, and we started cleaning. Honestly, that was a living parable for my life in the months and years to come. I thought, even then, *God is cleaning up my life.*

Indeed, I walked away from that crazy lifestyle, from the debauchery, the heavy partying, the smoking, the fornication… it all went. Amazingly enough, however, what I really struggled with was my identity as a son of God. Like the Prodigal Son, I would have been okay with living as a servant rather than a son. I wasn't ready to accept the responsibility of all that came with being His son—the exchanging of His plans for my plans. I wanted to punch the clock and go home. I'd go to church, do my Christian thing over here, and have my plan, my band, my music over there. I wanted compartmentalization. It was personal discipleship that enabled me to work through these issues. I had more experienced Christians in my life, teaching me, guiding me, helping me discover and embrace what it means to be a child of God.

This process of helping people through their issues, and aiding them in their discovery of their role and responsibilities as sons and daughters of God is where discipleship lives. The most impacting discipleship is a personal, role-up-your-sleeves, messy entanglement in other people's lives. Dave and Shelby, young in their own faith, sat with me almost every night and discipled me. They listened patiently to my objections and complaints; they walked with me through the Word as best they could; they prayed with me; they were forgiving when my frustrations boiled over into insults. Their discipleship meant everything to me. You don't have to have every answer, have a Bible College degree, be a certain age, or have a particular title in order to disciple people, but one thing you do need, something Dave and Shelby consistently demonstrated, is the heart of the Father.

4

 HEART OF THE BROTHER

Luke 15:25-32

"Now his older son was in the field. And as he came and drew near to the house, he heard music and dancing. So he called one of the servants and asked what these things meant. And he said to him, 'Your brother has come, and because he has received him safe and sound, your father has killed the fatted calf.'

"But he was angry and would not go in. Therefore his father came out and pleaded with him. So he answered and said to his father, 'Lo, these many years I have been serving you; I never transgressed your commandment at any time; and yet you never gave me a young goat, that I might make merry with my friends. But as soon as this son of yours came, who has devoured your livelihood with harlots, you killed the fatted calf for him.'

"And he said to him, 'Son, you are always with me, and all that I have is yours. It was right that we should make merry and be glad, for your brother was dead and is alive again, and was lost and is found.'"

There are two brothers in the Parable of the Lost Son: The irresponsible wild and crazy younger son, and the faithful, responsible, hardworking older son. And, yet, the older son gets the bad rap.

It's easy to recognize how the parable of the prodigal son is meant to speak to the "sinners and tax-collectors," who are surrounding Jesus. They are all "prodigal sons," who, coming to themselves, have returned home to their Heavenly Father. They've drawn near to Jesus to be taught. To them, this parable has a powerful message. You are welcome here; you can be forgiven; your Father in heaven has been longing for you; you were lost, but are found, and God is elated over it, and all the hosts of heaven with Him.

What about the rest of Jesus' audience, however, those to whom the parable is immediately addressed? What about the older brother? Don't we easily mistake this parable about the heart of the father for the younger son alone? In doing so, can't we get myopic in our approach to discipleship? Our tendency is to make the homebody angry brother represent the Pharisees... whom we hate and hold in disdain, "woe unto you" and all that. When reading this parable, we can carry this disdain with us. It's easy, in fact, to scan through our Christian relationships with our Pharisee radar on high, set to "Seek and Destroy." Some people make an easy target. More than a few solid Christians struggle in their relationships with overtly sinful people, and seem overly protective of the church culture. The question is, does Jesus use his parable to do this?

When using one of Jesus' parables, we need to distinguish between that which we wrench inappropriately out of a parable and that which falls out of the parable naturally given the culture in which it is told. At the risk of over analyzing The Parable of the Lost Son, we should at least recognize: 1. The Pharisees are not all villains. The people loved them. Many of them were good people who believed in Jesus. 2. Jesus' audience (the older and younger brothers) are more than just the Pharisees and sinners; there are also a host of those falling in-between ...like the disciples themselves. 3. The father in the parable has a certain tenderness toward the older brother. The father loves the stubborn fool. He goes out to him to win him, just as he went out to the younger brother to welcome him home.

How, then, do *we* win the older brother to discipleship? The father in the parable shows us the way:

- The father validates his worth and work.
- The father acknowledges and eases his fears about the Prodigal's return.
- The father coaxes him kindly to share his own heart toward his brother.

VALIDATING THE WORTH & WORK OF OLDER BROTHER

Andrew:

The older son is not just whistling Dixie when he speaks of his labors; he comes from the field in the midst of a full-blown party. They were celebrating while he was still working holding down the fort, so to speak. Guests had already arrived, music was in full swing, raw and recently mooing food was already cooking. He's been working in the field and under his labors the family has been prosperous, even when the region in which the younger brother had been traveling was in famine.

I know that it's not fashionable to admit this, but I have a warm place in my heart for the older brother. Indeed, I AM the older brother, at least in part. I'm the guy who, while far from perfect, grew up in the church, got saved at 5, spent my life in youth group, church, and our church's weekend coffee house, after a short period of rather vanilla confusion and doubt had an overwhelming and invigorating recommitment of my life 16 year old life to Christ, went to Bible college, waited until marriage to have sex, married a woman of equal faith who also waited, have worked consistently in the ministry, got my master's degree, got another master's degree while teaching at a Bible college, did a PhD, started a Bible college in India, yada, yada, yada.

I'm a firm believer in the power of the "older brother," as was Jesus and Paul. Jesus was the older brother on steroids, if a bit more welcoming of the prodigal than he, already having the heart of the Father—Sinless life, devout, stable and true. Paul was the "older brother" without caveat—"circumcised on the eighth day, of the people of Israel, of the tribe of Benjamin, a Hebrew of Hebrews; as to the law, a Pharisee; as to zeal, a persecutor of the church; as to righteousness under the law, blameless" (Philippians 3:5-6). Jesus praised many an older brother type saying, "Therefore every scribe who has been trained for the kingdom of heaven is like a master of a house, who brings out of his treasure what is new and what is old," (Matthew 13:52). Peter was the older brother, a rock for Jesus, jagged as he was. So was Andrew, James, John, and more than a few of the others, like Barnabas and Jesus' brothers who became powerhouses in the early church. Paul focused on the "older brothers" whenever he tried to penetrate a new community, going first to the Jews to win them, and turning to the gentiles only after he'd secured some of these "older brothers" for Jesus. "Older brothers" are stable, dependable, and devout; they provide instant leadership (Acts 13; Acts 17:1-4). A Bible saturated culture, mind and history make rich soil for the seed of the gospel, and an indispensable foundation for church stability.

So… Thank you, Older Brothers, for your service; we couldn't have done it without you!

ACKNOWLEGING & EASING OLDER BROTHER FEARS

I also understand the older brother's pain and fear. The younger brother's empty-handed reappearance is a threat to the older brother's inheritance, a severe disturbance to the established order of a disciplined farm. The father tells him, "All that I have is yours," but at that very moment that rascal of a brother of his is feasting on part of that "all" and is wearing an expensive array of still more. What's next? The older son is not necessarily a bad man (whatever we may import into him from the Pharisees), he has just grievances, and the father is gentile with him in his corrections. Indeed, we make a mistake by importing Jesus' "Woe-unto-you" rage into this exchange. The parable itself is, comparatively, a gentle correction, nudging their consciences toward a better reflection of the heart of the Father.

"Older brothers" tend to have a different vision of church than some ex-prodigals do, or those who are myopically fixated on prodigals.

In one vision, the church is a *sacred community*, a safe place for Christians to gather with like-minded souls, a family that can be trusted... not perfect, but a recognizable home in which to raise their kids and protect them from the ravages of a godless world. Evangelism is outreach to sinners and tax-collectors, working overtime to amalgamate those who "come to" themselves into the way of Christ and the culture of church.

I've been to that church. It's nice, if a bit rigid at times. Their preserve-this-place hearts gravitate toward 1 Corinthians 5:11, *"But now I am writing to you not to associate with anyone who bears the name of brother if he is guilty of sexual immorality or greed, or is an idolater, reviler, drunkard, or swindler—not even to eat with such a one."*

In another vision, the church is a *hospital* (if not a mental ward) for people severely damaged by sin; a hospital run by stable older brother types and transformed prodigals who do everything in their power to "bring in" the sinners and tax-collectors, to win them, and to disciple them.

I've been there too. It's awkward for me and more than a little chaotic at times, resembling the Corinthian church a lot more than the upper room. Their thou-shalt-not-judge hearts gravitate to most of what is around I Corinthians 5:11—*"I wrote to you in my letter not to associate with sexually immoral people—not at all meaning the sexually immoral of this world, or the greedy and swindlers, or idolaters, since then you would need to go out of the world. ...For what have I to do with judging outsiders? ...God judges those outside."* In this vision, however, "outside" isn't the walls of the church institution, but an intangible divide between "saved" and "lost."

The church services are a potpourri of saved, seeking, and desperately broken, but hoping souls.

The *sacred community* visionaries know that while "all sin is sin" in terms of separating a person from God, not all sin is the same in the real world of human interaction. Some sin is so damaging in its impact on heart and mind and body that it greatly complicates the process of discipleship, is excruciating to overcome, and seriously reduces expectations for usefulness in future ministry. Thank the Lord that he often exceeds our expectations.

The *hospital* visionaries are often so outwardly focused that they prove careless about the inward life of a congregation, and overlook "the little ones" from Matthew 18:6. *"Whoever causes one of these little ones who believe in Me to sin, it would be better for him if a millstone were hung around his neck, and he were drowned in the depth of the sea."* Some can be so myopic about championing the cause of the "younger brother" that they ignore the concerns—and at times the safety—of the "older brother"... especially if those "older brothers" are impressionable children.

The prodigal son is often more glamourous as an idea than as an intimate. We love their testimonies, such powerful witnesses to the grace of God and the power of the gospel to transform, but having to share a church with many of them can exasperate and threaten. Whatever the hospital visionaries may try to make us feel about the prodigals' presence in our services and in-church programs, one should know the real life consequences of certain types of ministry, of discipling certain types of people, the marrow deep depravity that fills certain types of sinners, and warps them at their human core. We shouldn't ignore these realities in a myopia of grace, and a Pollyanna perception of forgiveness in Jesus.

Let me provide a few real life examples of what I'm talking about.

My father was an elder in his church and had a heart for the hurting. He went to a Christian conference in a major city near our home one Saturday and met a homeless man who seemed so ill that my father could not leave him there. He loaded the semi-conscious man into the back seat of his car and brought him home. The homeless man eventually dried out and prayed the "sinner's prayer," but also turned out to be permanently brain damaged from drugs and a failed suicide attempt. He was schizophrenic and demon possessed. He saw visions of figures who encouraged him toward acts of evil, blasphemed Jesus Christ, and spewed hatred at the church and Christians trying to help him when under its influence. Yes, my father (Lord, bless his heart) took him home to sleep on the couch in our house with my 16 year old sister and me and my two brothers, ages 15, 13, & 11. He left for work that following Monday with this man still in the house with his wife and children who were home for summer vacation.

Meet "Mike." Mike was the pastor of a thriving church in a troubled community. Mike implemented an aggressive campaign to bring in the lost, hurting and broken from the highways and byways. It was wildly successful, significantly enlarging his congregation and youth group, but one of the elders came to him and said... I paraphrase, of course... "We made such and such plan, and pulled it off. We couldn't have asked for a better result. I couldn't be happier, but I'm leaving." Mike was aghast. "Leaving? Why would you leave?" The elder said, "Those people are destroying my children. They are undisciplined and immoral and have introduced my kids to horrible things. Their very faith is in danger."

One set of parents converted to Christ and brought their a-moral children with them to my wife's childhood congregation. She found a note left in a pew-Bible by one of the mid-teen daughters a few weeks into their attendance. It listed the married men in the church that she intended to seduce... she proved adept at it, destroying more than one marriage.

These, and stories like these, can become the fears of the "older brothers," and we ought to, like the father in the Parable of the Prodigal Son, acknowledge their concerns and act wisely.

We have a hosts of chronic substance abusers and addicts, who've spent their entire lives in the deceitful and manipulative paradigms of those conditions, many proving barely able to function at even basic levels of self-sufficiency, even after they come to Christ. We have the mentally ill, who could drain away the energy of a dozen fulltime ministers without seeming to improve. We will encounter these and many like them, people who have dark histories and ugly habits of mind and body. They are won to Christ and want help, but they have a treacherous road of sanctification ahead of them and are in need of aggressive and disciplined discipleship. People whose moral warehouses are empty, lacking what most would consider basic human decencies. Being passionate for Jesus doesn't instantly rectify poor upbringing, trauma, and lifelong habit.

When *hospital* visionaries scorn the *sanctified community* churches for a failure to make prodigals feel welcome and loved, they often fail to do so with an understanding of what they are asking. They frequently do so with a recklessness that fails to take the fallout seriously. It is easy to demand that others do things when it is they and not you who will pay the cost.

Why do I say all this? Because there is an important appeal that Jesus makes to all those standing outside the house, judging Jesus for his open acceptance of that crowd of tax-gatherers and sinners, betrayers and dysfunctional ones, and we can't fully understand it or implement it unless we do so with our eyes open, counting the cost, so to speak.

We have a great commission and we need wisdom and not just gospel passion to fulfill it.

SHARING THE HEART OF THE FATHER

In the parable, and in the billions of analogous situations that we find in the real world, the Father loves both of his sons. Does the "older brother" imagine for one second that the father's love is based on deeds? That he can earn the father's love because he stayed and worked and enlarged his inheritance, while his brother forsook them all and squandered his? Deeds may affect a parent's capacity for intimacy with a child, but love is deep and profound no matter what a child does. The Father is not blind to the realities involved in loving each, in satisfying his desire to be in harmonious relationship with each, but his love is powerful and painful and always hoping just the same. "*Son, you are always with me, and all that I have is yours,*" says the father to his older son, BUT, "*It was right that we should make merry and be glad, for your brother was dead and is alive again, and was lost and is found.*"

The older brother's reaction is self-serving, self-inflated, self-preserving. He claims, "All these years I've been serving you," but his reaction suggests something else. His brother disgusts him. He imagines himself of more value in the father's eyes, and is insulted to discover the fiction. He cares little about how broken hearted the father has been, knowing that his youngest son, whom he loves with all his heart, is out there somewhere, doing who knows what with who knows whom, maybe dead, maybe alive, corrupting himself, damaging his soul. If the older brother is really serving the father, his father's heart would matter to him, his father's pain would be his own pain, his father's longing his own greatest desire.

We cannot stand before the Holy Creator of All, claiming to love Him and serve Him without caring about what he cares about, loving what He loves, hating what he hates. Every man, woman, and child on this earth, every nation, tribe, and tongue, rich or poor, lost or found is an object of Divine love and concern. There is a real world distinction between life in the "upper-room" and life in the "Corinthian church," and both have their strengths and weaknesses, both reflect aspects of God's mission for the church, His divine vision being something better than both. We need to embrace all of I Corinthians 5:9-13.

> *I wrote to you in my letter not to associate with sexually immoral people—not at all meaning the sexually immoral of this world, or the greedy and swindlers, or idolaters, since then you would need to go out of the world. But now I am writing to you not to associate with anyone who bears the name of brother if he is guilty of sexual immorality or greed, or is an idolater, reviler, drunkard, or swindler—not even to eat with such a one. For what have I to do with judging outsiders? Is it not those inside the church whom you are to judge? God judges those outside. Purge the evil person from among you.*

The *sacred community* type church is awesome, but it's only the church if its doing what Christ commissioned the church to do… GO!

The "older brothers" are strong, stable, and essential, but they are only serving the Father if their own hearts are broken by what breaks His. If we have lost the heart of the Heavenly Father, we are useless in building His Kingdom; we are not serving Him, but only ourselves. We must love God and love what God loves… and God loves even the most despicable among us. Their lostness wounds Him. Their darkness breaks His heart.

We must each stand before Him in all His holiness, a creature before its creator, a creature in a sea of His creatures, none worthy of His love, all equal objects of His grace and mercy. We are called to preserve the Christian community, to judge it, train it, disciple it, but, without this foundation of love, we are like noisy gongs and clanging symbols.

44

5

FOLLOW ME & I'LL MAKE YOU

Matthew 4:19 *ESV*

Jesus said to them, "Follow Me
and I will make you fishers of men."

Jonathan:

Jesus was the greatest disciple-maker that ever lived. He spent three years with twelve guys—twelve regular, JV, blue-collared, roughneck dudes and through these ordinary men, He changed the world. It is a wonder, a marvel and a great testimony to the sheer power of personal discipleship. When we look at the backgrounds, the resumes of these men, it's surprising that anything was accomplished after Christ left planet earth. Matthew was a tax collector, Peter and Andrew, James and John were fishermen, Simon was a hot-headed zealot, none were qualified to build the Church and I think that's just the way Jesus wanted it. In fact it seems as though it was His intention to build His Church, His Kingdom on earth with the ordinary in order to display the extraordinary power of God. He doesn't call the qualified, but He qualifies the called. Jesus does the work. He sends the Holy Spirit to empower ordinary men and women to accomplish the extraordinary work of building the Kingdom of God.

The Disciples of Jesus didn't realize it at the time, but they were being trained and groomed to continue the work, to carry the torch that Jesus set on fire. When it was their turn, they realized how all of those lessons would pay off. It reminds me of the movie the Karate Kid. Here is this weak scrawny kid trying not to get beat up by the tough kids at school, but keeps finding his face bruised and in the dirt. Enter Mr. Miagi, a quiet old man from the island of Okinawa. One time when the tough kids are pummeling the scrawny weak kid, Mr. Miagi comes to his rescue, revealing that this quiet old man, he is actually a karate master! Scrawny weak kid asks that Mr. Miagi train him and so he does, but it's not what is expected. The days of his training are spent waxing the old man's car, painting his fence, and sanding his floor. Thinking that he is just being taken, used as the old man's chore boy, certainly not being trained in karate, scrawny weak kid gets upset (he does that a lot in the movie). So the old man shows him what he'd actually been learning *was* the fundamentals of karate. All along while scrawny weak kid was painting up and down, sanding in circles, waxing back and forth, his arms and wrists were being strengthened to become ridged defensive weapons. It's a great movie, I saw it a million times as a kid, made me take karate lessons, I made it to purple belt.

So, here is Jesus. One fine day, He's walking along the seaside and spies two fishermen mending their nets. He calls to them and says, *"Follow Me and I will make you fishers of men"* (Matthew 4:19). In this call, we can see a kind of blueprint, perhaps a formula for disciple-making. Though I don't believe in any one formula for disciple-making, this phrase creates a good paradigm for us. It's a good 1,2,3 process—*1. Follow Me, 2. I will make you, 3. Fishers of men*. This is a model that we can use ourselves to help us to become great disciple-makers. Let's look at it a little closer.

1. FOLLOW ME

A good disciple-maker is one who can be followed. It's pretty simple right? If I followed you around everyday for three years, would I be more like Jesus in the end? These men did just that. They followed Jesus, they observed how He loved the lost, healed the sick and dealt with the prideful, the religious elite, the crowds, the children, the Gentiles, the sinners, the saints, how He handled criticism and finally how He suffered. They watched, they learned and in some cases they participated... they waxed His car, painted His fence, sanded His floor, ran for donkeys... and when it was their turn, they were empowered by the Holy Spirit to follow the example that they witnessed first hand from following Jesus.

As Jesus chose His disciples, so ought we. I realized early in my Christian walk that I needed to have some guys that I could point to and say, "These are my guys." I believe that the Holy Spirit puts people in our paths, on our hearts, people to come along side of, to work with, to raise up, to allow in our lives in a close way, to teach, to train, to disciple. So the questions become: "Are you someone who can be followed?" "Who is following you?" "What are they learning?"

2. I WILL MAKE YOU

When Jesus says, "I will make you," what He is actually doing is putting Himself on the hook. He is committing to them, committing to make something of them. Here is where I believe we drop the ball... big-time, committing to others. It's the big C word right? COMMITMENT. Ugh... This means spending our all too precious time with others, answering the phone when they call, getting into their mess, etc. Yes. Committing to others in a discipleship relationship is where the heavy lifting really comes in. It's a big and often messy work. Committing to someone to raise them up in the Lord can be daunting and for some, downright hair raising.

Britney and I currently get the privilege of traveling full-time and every week we are at a different church teaching on this subject of personal disciple-making and challenging congregations to make disciples. When it comes to this point of commitment, we often hear—I don't feel qualified.

People are insecure about their own abilities. These insecurities can come from a host of sources, They don't feel they know enough, don't feel stable enough, don't feel virtuous enough. They don't feel they enough time, enough discipline, enough commitment and the like. Pardon the redundancy, but God doesn't call the qualified, but He qualifies the called. We don't have to have all of the answers to make disciples; we don't have to be perfect people, have Bible degrees, be a pastor, have a title in the church; we just have to be filled with the Holy Spirit and have the loving heart of the Father for others.

During his first master's, Andrew asked a Hebrew professor he met, "When do you reach a point where you feel really comfortable with Hebrew?" His answer astonished him. The Prof said, "After you've taught it a few times." Indeed, dedicating yourself to discipling another is often the best impetus to becoming all the things you knew you should have been before deciding to disciple someone in the first place. In other words, taking on responsibility for another often supplies a sense of duty to compensate for what has been lacking in your own levels of personal discipline, whether educationally, temptation-ally, or commitment-ally.

Remember Dave and Shelby, my guitar player and his wife? They sat with me nearly every night. They discipled me, but they were only three months in the Lord themselves. What I learned by this is that you don't have to know everything, but perhaps just stay a few lessons ahead ☺. Dave and Shelby showed me a good example of what a disciple-maker looks like. They were there for me. They let me know that they were committed to me, and that made all the difference in the world. Perhaps they didn't give me all the right answers, weren't perfect, and maybe they didn't do everything right, but they loved me and made my spiritual growth a priority in their own spiritual growth. Discipling me forced them to seek answers and discipleship from others so they would not fail me. They taught me what they knew, prayed for me and helped me grow at my own pace. For this, I am eternally grateful for them.

3. FISHERS OF MEN

Telling these fishermen that He would make them fishers-*of*-men was Jesus' way of giving His disciples a new vision for their lives. They would become His soul-winners, His disciple-makers, His Kingdom builders. That's a pretty big vision, especially considering to whom He is saying it. Remember, these guys weren't exactly playing on the varsity team, but He chose to use them and use what they knew as an analogy for their new lives—fishing. Rather than being people who spend their days catching fish for their livelihood, they would spend their lives catching people for the Kingdom.

Before I was a Christian, I was as selfish as the day is long. I didn't even care for the people I claimed to love. When I came to Christ, however, part of my transformation was a surprising and hitherto unknown concern even for strangers. The love of God entered into my heart and out again for others. Part of disciple-making is loving others enough to help them see the vision that God has for them as disciples and as His disciple-makers. When we come to Christ, He gives us a new heart, a new purpose, a new life commission, a new desire that the lost be found, and that spiritual infants grow big and strong in Christ. Raw desire is not enough, however. He equips us for this great commission by His Holy Spirit and sends others to help us along our journey as well. In this way we become His fishers of men.

Sounds great, right? Evidently, it isn't that simple. If it were, we wouldn't be writing this book, disciple-making would be the Christian norm, and vast numbers of de-churched wouldn't be de-churched. There's a breakdown somewhere, a short-circuit of what should be our innate spiritual inclination.

JIMMY

My friends all took off soon after I came to Christ. I suppose Jesus freaks are annoying. Dave and Shelby moved on to another church, but I stayed there in that small New England church for months as the only one in his 20's... then Jimmy walked through the doors. He was a High School acquaintance of mine. "Jimmmmmmy!" We became fast friends whether he liked it or not. I think I head locked him. He had just given his life to Christ and he had come out of the same lifestyle I had. So... I knew from recent personal experience that he would need someone to help him, to be there for him, to... well... disciple him.

Jimmy and I spent lots of time together. I taught him what I knew; we walked through the Bible together; I helped him to pray; answered many questions best I could, sought answers for those I couldn't. I wanted to be there for Jimmy as Dave and Shelby were there for me. Soon, Jimmy's cousin Fil came to Christ. Then, it was me Jimmy and Fil... the Peter James and John of Grace Chapel. We became inseparable, and, one-by-one, others came. Soon, Jimmy and Fil's house was packed almost every night with young men and women, praying for each other, reading the Bible, talking and being discipled.

We had then, what would now be called "a small group," and we were quickly growing into small groups. As I devoted more time to my studies at Bible college, Jimmy, Fil and others each began attracting eager young Christians into their own orbit for a time. It wasn't forced; it wasn't programmatic; it wasn't "Six Steps to a Successful Small Group." It was organic; it was excitement; it was relational; it was community. It was a spontaneous spiritual dedication to each other as eager disciples seeking discipleship, and paying it forward in kind. It was a period of time in my life that showed me what vibrant small groups can be, what they can accomplish in the personal lives of Christians. Looking back, it seems amazing, but, at the time, we were just doing life together—normal Christianity as far as we knew.

When we see discipleship reduced to a program, a system, a set of classes to go through, or a church assimilation process, it just seems so artificial, so saccharin. Structure in a group or community is necessary, but structure ought to accommodate the community, not the community the structure. The Sabbath was made for man, not man for the Sabbath. Either we have a government for the people by the people or we have a people for the government by the government. Authority, doctrine, and organization are meant to keep a community stable and healthy, but too often the church and its programs become central rather than serviceable. "I have this program here and I need people to run it and fill it!!!" or "I have these people here and I need a plan to serve them."

This one of the primary factors for the bulk of the de-churched. When they feel policy trumps people, when the people are little more than fuel for the machine, they want out. They're done.

6

GOing Community

John 13:35

"By this all will know that you are My disciples,
if you have love for one another."

Britney:

I love the holidays. Growing up in my home meant celebrating *both* Jewish and Christian holidays… so LOTS of gifts! My dad is Jewish, born and bred in New York City, and my mom was raised Baptist in Northern Virginia. As a family of mixed faiths, living outside of Washington D.C., we celebrated Rosh Hashanah, Easter, Passover, Christmas, Hanukah and everything in between. Occasionally, my two younger brothers and I would attend church and temple, as well as Sunday school and Hebrew school. I grew up loving the holidays and traditions, because it meant family, fun, good food (or in some Jewish feasts, not so good food) and warm memories… except for the gefilte fish—*yuck!*

My understanding of faith, however, was limited. I remember a time in 4th grade when I asked a friend why we celebrated Christmas. He chuckled, confounded that I really didn't know, and told me it was Jesus' birthday—*Jesus? Oh…wait… does that mean there's no Santa Clause?*

When I was twelve years old, my world turned upside down. My parents divorced. It was a whirlwind year of custody disputes, counseling sessions, confusion and heartache. The next thing I knew, my mother had custody of me, my father had custody of my two brothers, and I was living with my mom, my brand new stepfather and stepbrother in Massachusetts, and enrolled in an Assemblies of God Christian private school, of all places. In the blink of an eye... new home, new family, new school, new classmates, new brand of religion... not exactly a comfortable situation.

BUT THEN GOD

During my first couple weeks of school, my classmates and I went on a retreat, spending a few days at a beautiful campground in Massachusetts. We participated in games and team-building activities during the day, and chapel services at night. Even so, I was heartsick and angry, still reeling from all the newness and loss.

I went to chapel my first night with great hesitation. I had no earthly idea what to expect. It was awkward enough that I was the new kid in school without friends, or a sense of belonging, wearing an unfamiliar school uniform, but, now, I had to huddle in a small wooden chapel in the woods of New England, singing spiritual songs that everyone else seemed to know except for me. You'd think that this experience would have sent me running over the river and through the woods... *Grandma's house, here I come!*

I don't remember the message that was preached that night, nor do I remember the songs that we sang, but what I do remember, what is forever engraved in my mind and heart, is that I felt like Jesus introduced Himself to me, extending His arms and calling me by name. As we sang, an overwhelming sense of love and peace like I had never experienced before enveloped me. It wasn't a fleeting emotional response aroused by the music or atmosphere, but it was an undeniable force overtaking me... I began weeping. My trembling hands rose instinctively like a child reaching for Father. I could almost hear

Him tell me that He knew me, He loved me, and He was with me. That moment changed me forever. The insecure and displaced girl with the weight of the world on her shoulders who concealed anger and bitterness in her heart was NOT the same lighthearted girl who left that small wooden New England chapel that night, practically skipping out, embarrassingly so, because she was so joyful and free.

As amazing as this experience was, it was only the beginning of a beautiful journey of discovery that soon followed. My family and I were not attending church during this time, but my school quickly became like my church. I had a daily Bible class where I was taught the Word of God, and once a week we had chapel services at school where my love for the Lord grew in worship, and where I was challenged in my relationship with Christ. I started acquiring all the worship and Christian music I could get my hands on… which was a big deal, considering how much of my identity was wrapped up in the music I listened to. All I wanted was to be in the presence of God, and I turned my bedroom into a sanctuary where I surrendered myself in worship and where I read and learned to love God's Word.

In those years, the Lord brought a community of friends, teachers, and pastors into my life that showed me the love of God, and authentically demonstrated what it meant to be a follower of Christ. Whether they knew it or not, they were discipling me, but my family still didn't have a church we could call our own.

MY BIG FAT CHURCH FAMILY

I was sixteen when my family and I first attended Faith Assembly. In one visit, we knew we were home. The church wasn't located in the greatest area of town, and there wasn't anything particularly appealing about the building itself—a small, faded white New England church, complete with steeple and old stained glass windows. The building showed its age, but there was life and love in the hearts of the people.

We instantly felt comfortable… as if they were welcoming us into their living room. It was a church filled with authentic people–raw, honest, passionate, multi-cultural, fun loving people who genuinely cared for one another. It felt like a big family, led by a lively Italian pastor and his wife, who were engaging, caring, creative, free-spirited followers of Christ, committed to spreading the gospel and serving their local community.

It was here, in this humble New England church and youth group that my faith was further grounded as I was challenged to serve and grow in greater capacities. The older, more mature Christians acted as spiritual moms and dads. They spoke meaning and purpose into my life, and much like my own home, provided an environment that fostered my gifts and taught me how to use them for the kingdom of God.

More than just friends, the teenagers and young adults became like brothers and sisters. It was far more than a casual "see you next Sunday" kind of relationship we had with one another. We were whole-heartedly invested in each other's lives, dedicated to helping one another grow as disciples, and the bond we shared was strong.

The pastor had a particular passion for getting the youth actively involved in the work of the ministry at various levels, encouraging us to hone our talents and to stretch our limits. We were involved in worship teams, traveling music groups, dramas, evangelistic outreaches, etc. Busy? Yes. Growing together in Christ? Definitely.

COMMUNITY UNITY

Year after year, our Webstock weekend outdoor festival attracted visitors from all over New England. We held a myriad of different events and activities from basketball tournaments and face painting, to rap groups and worship concerts. Most events were homegrown ministries from our own church. We witnessed countless people respond to the gospel, even some of the news reporters that came out to cover the event!

It ended every year with celebratory baptisms, including my own, in the town lake, Lake Chargoggagoggmanchauggagogg-chaubunagungamaugg... no, I'm not kidding... it's the longest name for any place in the U.S., the sign is a huge arch over the whole road. The name is Native American for "You fish on your side; I fish on my side; nobody fish in the middle." I always found this oddly ironic—no compromise when following Christ, it's all or nothing! Maybe I'm being sentimental because it's where I was baptized.

Our impact within the town and surrounding areas started to grow. Pastor Rick befriended the local authorities, and before long, they too were coming to Christ and joining our church family. Prominent drug dealers in the town found themselves loved and embraced within our church community and gave their lives to Christ, becoming part of our active youth group. Church was exciting, and I was thrilled to be apart of it.

CREATING A GOing COMMUNITY

As an adult now, in full-time ministry, I can't help but look back on those incredible teenage years and reflect on what it was about those experiences that grounded me in my faith, when so many other millennials were falling away from the Lord. Some of the greatest lessons I've learned to this day about healthy church and discipleship-centered-Christian community stem from those early experiences.

I'd like to share a bulleted list of what I see as predominant factors that anchored me and helped me to grow as a disciple within my school and church community:

- The pastor and church leaders intentionally engaged youth culture.
- They demonstrated genuine care for us by taking the time to get to know us, our passions and talents.
- They intentionally found ways to creatively involve us in the work of the ministry.
- The leaders lived the gospel before us.
- Love should be at the core of everything we do.
- Aesthetics are important, as is excellence, but heart is key.
- Teamwork is vital—each member of the body is important—we all have something to contribute.
- Effective pastors and disciple-makers are great encouragers who see the potential in people and relentlessly speak life, hope and purpose into them.
- Christ-like community is magnetic and the greatest witness we have to the world around us. It must be continuously and intentionally created, cultivated, and promoted.

Discipleship happens in community. We're stronger and more effective together. A community can grow together, GO together and in doing so, fulfill the Great Commission together. I'm convinced that a vibrant, loving, growing, GOing community of passionate Christ followers is the most powerful force of good in the world. It demonstrates the love of God, His heart for His children and the power of His Spirit to restore and transform the lives of people.

Creating this kind of GOing community takes full intention, a love for God, a passion for people and a sincere heart to see Him move. When church feels more like family than a religious institution, or a corporation, it engages the despondent and the cynical of this generation and draws them into a life of passion and purpose. Speaking as a millennial, I can say that it is this type of community that my generation responds to and deeply desires, even if they don't realize it. Millennials want to rally around a cause that matters; they seek authentic relationship and they want to be a part of something bigger than themselves. A healthy, GOing community fulfills this. Creating a growing, GOing community of disciple-making disciples must be of the utmost importance in all that we do.

7

YOU FEED THEM

Matthew 14:16

Jesus said to them, "They do not need to go away.
You give them something to eat."

Jonathan:

They came from all over; thousands flocked to a desolate place to see Jesus, to hear His teachings, to witness the miracles, to be healed, to experience God. Five thousand men gathered, not counting the women and children. There, He taught them and healed them; they, essentially, had church, but then it grew late and the disciples, realizing that they didn't have enough food to feed them all, told Jesus to send the people away. Sometimes I wonder if we still are in this habit of sending away those that are left spiritually hungry and thirsty after our services have concluded. Jesus said to them, *"They do not need to go away. You give them something to eat"* *(Matthew 14:16)*. This was startling for them to hear, but Jesus, I believe, had more in mind in this statement, more than just physical nourishment. In true Jesus form, He uses the natural to teach the spiritual.

Here is the account according to Mark:

> *They went away in the boat to a desolate place by*
> *themselves. Now many saw them going and recognized*
> *them, and they ran there on foot from all the towns and got*
> *there ahead of them. When he went ashore he saw a great*
> *crowd, and he had compassion on them, because they were*

*like sheep without a shepherd. And he began to teach them
many things. And when it grew late, his disciples came to
him and said, 'This is a desolate place, and the hour is
now late. Send them away to go into the surrounding
countryside and villages and buy themselves something to
eat.' But he answered them, 'You give them something to
eat.' And they said to him, 'Shall we go and buy two
hundred denarii worth of bread and give it to them to
eat?' And he said to them, 'How many loaves do you
have? Go and see.' And when they had found out, they
said, 'Five, and two fish.' Then he commanded them all to
sit down in groups on the green grass. So they sat down in
groups, by hundreds and by fifties. And taking the five
loaves and the two fish he looked up to heaven and said a
blessing and broke the loaves and gave them to the disciples
to set before the people. And he divided the two fish among
them all. And they all ate and were satisfied. And they
took up twelve baskets full of broken pieces and of the
fish. And those who ate the loaves were five thousand men.*
(Mark 6: 32-44).

I wonder if there is an analogy here for the church. Jesus
had His leaders sit the people down into small groups; He
blessed the food, broke the bread and gave it to his leaders to
distribute to the groups. We could use this as a church model,
couldn't we? We could look at this and say, "See, Jesus believed
in small groups." This might seem a fanciful use of the text, but
would we be wrong? It *is* a great way to ensure that everyone in
our churches are spiritually fed. The pastor breaks the bread of
life and gives it to his leaders, who then distribute it to the
multitudes small, organized, manageable groups… pretty simple
analogy right? It may or may not have been Mark's specifically
intended take-away, but it certainly works, and is used as a
successful discipleship paradigm by many growing churches
today.

SMALL GROUP MODEL

Several years ago, I took a worship leader position at a prominent church in Florida. I was excited by the fact that so many seemed to be spiritually moved during our worship services, but there was a problem. We didn't offer much by way of purposeful discipleship for new converts. I'd be leading worship Sunday after Sunday, watching people commit their lives to Christ, feeling a little guilty, feeling like we were committing the Disciple's error—just sending them away. It was as if we were saying, "Okay, come back next Sunday for another service," rather than personally engaging these new believers, getting to know them and plugging them into a discipling relationship. Not only that, but we were a church full of untapped potential. The harvest was plentiful, but the laborers were in their pews. Seasoned Christians filled our services, rife with great testimony, tested wisdom, proven faith, natural and spiritual maturity, and, yet, they were not engaged. The Great Commission beckoned them from our alters, but they were not being rallied to meet it. It was heart breaking.

We needed to do something. I felt I needed to do something. We needed to create a way for the new believers to connect with the body. We needed to create opportunities and places for the church to GO and make disciples. I looked back. I looked back on my own early discipleship experiences, both giving and receiving… it all took place in small group settings. I petitioned the pastor and the board to allow me to start a discipleship small group ministry in addition to my duties as the worship leader. I researched different models, read book upon book on the topic. What I learned was that there is no magic pill, no one formula for small groups that will have the same results across the board. In all the books I'd read, I hadn't come across anything that gave a step-by-step method that fit with the culture of our church. I needed our groups to be unique to us, to our needs, to our church community. There are many of interesting small group paradigms—*affinity groups* (shared interest groups, like golf, knitting, etc.), *care groups* (shared problem groups, like single mothers, grief, recovery, etc.), *fellowship groups* (hang out sessions), *classes* (shared courses of study), *function groups* (prayer group, hospital visitation, community service, etc.). There are plenty of good books out there on building small groups; there are many pastors and leaders who have highly successful small group ministries. So, I make no claim here to have some definitive answer for your small group needs, but I have learned a few things from building a meaningful and multiplying discipleship based program from scratch. Perhaps its principles will prove beneficial to you in your own discipleship pursuits.

We had a big task ahead of us, to say the least, but I drew up a plan and wrote out my vision and presented it to the pastor and board. They agreed and we got started. At the time, there were a couple of existing small groups from our church that had been meeting for some 30 years together. They were good; they functioned as fellowship groups, they provided care for one another, but they were—whatever they would have claimed to the contrary—closed groups. I wanted to ensure that we created organically growing, naturally multiplying, discipleship based small groups. To borrow from an old fishing analogy, we had been catching and releasing, now we needed to catch, keep and clean them. I wanted to build baskets for the fish, places where we could direct new converts, small groups where they could be discipled on a regular basis. We devised a plan. It was our way to GO and make disciples in our community. We started by picking a few leaders and training them. The training was based mainly on how to effectively facilitate a discipleship based small group. It was sort of the do's and don'ts, what we'd learned from our experiences and studies on discipleship and how to practically and effectively lead a small group. These were the main components of the training.

1. Leaders should schedule meetings weekly.
2. Leaders should conduct meetings in predictable,

safe & comfortable environments.

3. Leaders should keep small groups small.
4. Leaders should groom future group leaders one on one.
5. Leaders should attend leadership meetings with other small group leaders regularly.
6. Leaders should facilitate conversationally based meetings. (See Chapter 8)
7. Leaders should work from Bible based curriculum. (See Chapter 9)

1. Leaders should schedule meetings weekly

We had a lot of conversations on whether or not groups could or should meet weekly or every other week. We concluded that it is important that these groups meet weekly in order to preserve the discipleship goals and, not merely, the fellowship qualities. If a new believer were to come to a group that met every other week, and miss a week, that would mean that he or she would go a month without meaningful, personal discipleship contact. This is way too long for young believers.

2. Leaders should conduct meetings in predictable, safe & comfortable environments.

The physical locations and the environments where meetings are held ought to feel safe. The houses or public places where groups meet should be conducive for conversation, free from major distractions and both casual and comfortable enough for people to want to return. People need to know what to expect when they come, and they should expect to find a safe, comfortable, and predictable environment conducive to intimate conversation about vital things in a judgement-free-zone.

Some of our groups found that creating a social contract proved helpful in creating a safe environment. Each of the members would voice their expectations for the group's dynamic. For example: 1. What is said in the group stays in the group, 2. Show mutual respect and kindness for all ideas, no matter how foolish they may seem, 3. No conversation hogging, 4. Be kind and respectful to each other. Sometimes these expectation were written down and the contract signed by everyone in the group. It forged a sense of group accountability and empowered the leader to contain runaway situations.

My group met on Tuesday nights at a local Starbucks. We sat outside on the patio, because inside the music was too loud… and, being a musician, this was far too distracting for me. Though Starbucks may seem like an unstable place to meet, with its constantly shifting clientele, differing employees, alternating seating arrangements, it was consistently so, and, therefore, expected, proving to be a safe environment for our group to meet. It wasn't long before we became "regulars." Some other regulars would pick up on the fact that we were openly sharing our beliefs without judgment, and felt comfortable enough to enter into the conversation. We welcomed them. In time, some of these folks actually joined our group.

Some groups and group models run quite successfully as closed groups, or in a closed environment, meeting with the same set of people for a set amount of time. I, however, welcomed outsiders into our group because I saw it as an evangelistic opportunity. It also, incidentally, proved to be a training opportunity for my group. They watched how I handled various differing ideas and beliefs, facilitating complex conversations, and they replicated that pattern when they eventually ran their own groups. Personally, I loved it and so did my guys. It was challenging; it was real, and it kept people excited and engaged. I'm not sure if I would encourage this public, welcoming-of-outsiders model for *all* small groups, but it worked for us.

3. Leaders should keep small groups small.

I don't believe in forcing a large group to split, or dictating to a group leader that he or she must divide. That said, I do believe in encouraging growing small groups to split in order to stay small. Splitting a growing small group, however, is one of the hardest things about this type of ministry. A group with thirty people in it, however, is more like a church than a small group. In our travels, we've had the chance to talk with more than a few pastors with 30-40 people in their Sunday morning services. Inevitably, we ask them, "Are you running small groups?" More often than not, they respond with, "Oh, we are a small group," ...then chuckle. We are rarely amused, however, when pastors of small churches misunderstand both the processes and the value of small group ministry. A church of this number still has the opportunity to grow large by growing small—To work in an old metaphor, think cell division in a growing organism.

There isn't a magic number that a group reaches that disqualifies it as a small group, but in our ministry, we took Jesus' example and focused on 12ish. Somewhere around there it starts to feel like a large meeting. When this happens, open sharing feels more like public speaking and this shuts down the more introverted and reserved folks. In order for everyone to have a say, no one gets to say much. These meetings can become more lecture oriented and, by necessity, heavily structured, thus, churchy.

I had a small group leader whose small group grew to about 40, all showing up at his home for their weekly meetings. The one problem was that they didn't want to split. The other problem was that the leader didn't have any perceived heir apparent... I should say heir apparents because, realistically, he could have divided into 5 groups. "It's not like a small group anymore," he said to me asking for help, "it's more like church... bad church." We worked together to find a solution. I sent trained leaders into this leader's group to try to build relationships with it members that would become and impetus to natural, healthy and willing division. Even so, nada. It was too artificial and didn't take. For a division to happen effectively it has to happen naturally.

4. Leaders should groom future group leaders one-on-one.

We asked the leaders that they meet with at least one person in their group on a one-on-one basis for more in-depth personal discipleship in order to raise them up as a future small group leaders when it comes time for the group to split. These would be people that the Lord would put on the hearts of the leaders.

This part was key. It replicated Jesus' inner-circle, the more intimate relationships he had with Peter, James and John. These were the next generation of leaders. The trainees would help the leader facilitate the group, then, when the leader felt the trainees were ready, they would lead the group under supervision, debriefing later in their one-on-ones. Eventually, the group would divide and some would follow the new leader. It replicated the discipleship pattern that Jesus shows us:

- Jesus did—the disciples watched
- Jesus did—the disciples helped
- The disciples did—Jesus watched
- The disciples did—Jesus left

Nothing accelerates learning like necessity. You don't wait for a future leader to be perfect before letting them lead. They will grow faster when placed into the pressure cooker of leading. A pressure cooker should always be watched, however. When I first asked Keith (Chapter 1) to lead a group he studied super hard and then spoke for 90 minutes straight. I didn't interrupt because I didn't want to embarrass him in front of the others, but, in our one-on-one time, I reiterated the importance of conversational discipleship. It took him a little while to get used to asking and listening. In his mind, he was the teacher, which meant that he did all of the talking. I modeled facilitation, but his nerves would kick in and his mouth would follow. He got the hang of it eventually, but it took coaching. The pressure of needing to lead caused him to study harder, to grow more dependent on the Lord, and to adapt his leadership style. His growth was exponential.

This highlights part of the natural division failure of our earlier story (See #3 above). The leader, as good as he was, didn't raise up anyone to succeed him. For good or for ill, there wasn't anyone in the group that he trusted as a future leader. Therefore he refused to have one-on-ones with anyone to give them a chance to develop into a potential leader.

This paradigm of field training for small group leaders provided a vital accountability structure for efficient growth. When people would approach me about leading a small group, I simply plugged them into an existing group and trusted my leaders to provide the necessary, example, training and evaluation for future leaders and their new small groups. We compensated for any corrosion or dilution in the making-a-copy-of-a-copy process with number 5.

5. Leaders should attend leadership meetings with other small group leaders regularly.

We required our leaders to commit to meet once a month with all the other small group leaders. We held this meeting after a church service to avoid taking up another valuable night in our busy leader's lives. This meeting provided a modicum of small group training, gave a sense of solidarity among the leaders and offered a safe place where basic issues could be addressed and war wounds could be mended. I structured the meeting much like I would any small group. I provided a small training portion to start the meeting, opened it up for dialogue, then we allowed time for house cleaning. The leaders were encouraged to talk about what we called the ministry and the monster parts of the small groups. The ministry portion dealt with what God was doing in their groups, the testimonies, the new leaders, progress of new groups and members. The monster part dealt with the things needing fixing, issues needing addressing. It's important to note here that no confidential information about group members was shared in these meeting.

6. Leaders should facilitate conversationally based meetings

We wanted our discipleship groups to be conversational rather than lecture or church service-y. I wanted the groups to be a place where people could talk openly about their spiritual needs, a place where they could ask hard questions without condemnation. Both in experience and research, we believed that people learn best when they are able to share openly and honestly about their issues, struggles, doubts, beliefs, disbeliefs, etc, and how do you disciple someone when everything that's really going on in their hearts, minds and lives is held back, or secret? Who is going to open up if they believe that doing so will expose them to ridicule, contempt, judgment, condemnation, ostracism, or the like… not me. As much as I like a good debate, I'm not a glutton for punishment. People need to feel secure in order to speak plainly about their circumstances and concerns. This being the case, we wanted our leaders to act more like well-prepared facilitators than lecturers and know-it-alls; they were encouraged to do lots of listening and asking, and not dominate the conversation.

In studying the de-churched (discussed in chapter 2), we discovered that many church refugees are desperately seeking interaction in a spiritual community; they're looking to discover and experience God in meaningful conversation and growing relationships. When they didn't find it in church, they checked out. This suggests that, had they found authentic conversation, had they found meaningful relationship, they may have remained in the church. We wanted to prepare our leaders to facilitate these very conversations. They needed to be able to keep a group discussion on track, on topic, but not in such a way as to squash or squelch participation and honesty. (More on this in Chapter 8.)

7. Leaders should work from Bible based curriculum.

I wanted the leaders to work with simple, Bible based curriculum. I would let them choose the curriculum that best fit the personality of their group, but it would have to be approved. The approval process was pretty simple and fast: the teaching needed be Biblically sound, teach the fundamentals, have an easily digestible structure, and give achievable and timely goals. We wanted some of the goals to emerge from the spiritual expectations of the group members themselves. We felt that a set of measures kept the group focused on its purposeful existence beyond its social value.

An often overlooked and seriously undervalued component to discipleship relates to this issue of discipleship content, particularly in relation to training qualified leaders. Time, like anything else is a limited resource that needs to be carefully managed. Unfortunately, it seems to me (Andrew) that the limited amount of time that many Christians are willing to expend on getting vital training in a variety of areas has set the stage for our age's educational expectations in leadership training. We have become minimalists where we should be passionate expansionists. We accept mastery of pre-prepared lessons from others as a legitimate replacement for mastery of life's and Scripture's subject matter. In chapter X, therefore, I will establish a guiding star trajectory for leadership training that goes far beyond the minimalist qualifications for running a small group meeting based on pre-packaged curriculum and establish a map for a life-long journey into ever-expanding, ever-deepening biblical and theological competence.

A NOTE ON GENDER

While not a part of our original training, we learned a few things about gender and small groups along the way that proved beneficial. Some of our groups were mixed groups (both men and women). Since our small group model focused on discipleship, (as opposed to fellowship groups, shared interest groups, or care groups) these mixed groups came with specific challenges to the discipleship process. The sexual tension between singles was a constant distraction. Will a single young man open up as needed in front of a young lady he hopes to impress? For that matter, will a husband or wife truly open up about his or her personal issues when doing so may cause distrust, disgust, jealousy, injured pride, and hurt feelings between them. Mixed groups tended not only to bloat quickly, adding couples rather than individuals, but they also tended, based on the shallower discussions to gravitate toward social meetings or churchy meetings. As such they were difficult to divide in healthy discipleship expansion. We are definitely not against these types of groups, but they did tend to defy our purposes in establishing discipleship based small groups.

In discipleship relationships, we believe it best that men disciple men and women disciple woman. Men and women have their own respective issues and it's often best when "never the twain shall meet." It comes down to safety, effectiveness and openness, as discussed in #2 and #6 above. Men feel safer sharing their personal struggles with sin and temptation with other men, as women do with other women. Gender specific groups make the discipleship process safer, more open and, consequently, more effective.

MY GROUP

This is how I ran my weekly group. We would get together Tuesday nights at Starbucks, order stuff, and start around 7:00pm. We'd talk openly for about ten minutes, giving late-comers a chance to get settled. If there was a new person attending the group, we would do what we would called our "one-minutes." I'd have each person would take turns talking for one-minute about who they are and how they joined the group. This gave everyone a chance to say a little something about themselves and warmed everyone up to each other. Inevitably people would go over the one-minute, so I would have to move it along. Then I would open with prayer and about 15-20 minutes of a lesson. This included reading a scripture, reading a part of the lesson and discussing the subject from my own perspective. Then I would start asking questions from the lesson.

In my preparation time before the meeting, I would go over these questions and answer them for myself. I would often have things I'd discover and like to say, personal stories, but I would hold off and wait to see if they would come up naturally within the group conversation. More often than not, that's exactly what would happen.

I would try to keep the ball moving, the conversation flowing. I'd do my best to draw out those who were more reserved and my equal best to good naturedly contain those who tended to dominate the discussion. I wanted participation from all without giving the sense of controlling the dialogue. By asking the questions, I was able to do both. It's good to remember that people learn best when they are able to talk, so facilitating the conversation was the goal.

For my group, I wanted structure without formality, unity without uniformity and organic openness without confusing conversation. It's the facilitator's job to stay on topic, but be open enough to let the discussion be organic enough and natural enough to go where it needs to. This does take time to get used to if the leader is new, which is why it is vital that new group leaders be a part of a group so they can get a feel for how the groups function.

So how are we GOing and making disciples within a group? Where does discipleship come in? It comes with the discussion, with the lessons, and the questions surrounding the subject matter. It comes in when people are able to openly and safely talk about their issues, their doubts, their struggles. It comes with being an example, because it comes in the watching. I'm of the belief that in discipleship, people learn by watching the discipler. They watch how they handle themselves in various situations, how they handle objections, disagreements, people with needs, how they pray, how they carry themselves, their temperament, how they control their emotions. There are a lot of tests that come up for the leader in a group dynamic and people watch how we handle each of them. More often than not, people learn more by what we do than what we say.

8

CONVERSATIONAL DISCIPLESHIP

1 Thessalonians 5:11 *ESV*

*Therefore comfort each other and edify one another,
just as you also are doing.*

Studies among the 100 million plus de-churched people in America list a lack of effective and honest discussion as a constant claim for their departure. The de-churched feel pressured to conform to a system of beliefs without room for debate, or even a place to voice concerns, or differing perspectives. It is either believe or leave and, so, they leave. Weather or not every church refugee's claim to this is valid, the reality of the claim is just. All three of us have witnessed this throughout our ministries and travels. This as a tragedy, but it is also where small groups come in—big-time.

Church services create a formal atmosphere. They become events for people to receive, to sit and to listen. Small groups provide a place for people to talk back, to discuss their views, voice their doubts and frustrations, what they believe or don't believe, to work out problems, to build relationships with people who care to listen. This is what many people are looking for; hey, it's what I'm looking for—a conversational place where ideas can be discussed safely.

In a church setting, formality can be both a blessing and a curse. On one hand you need formality to have a service, you need order and structure; on the other hand, formality creates space between people. In a formal atmosphere, conversation is usually little more than small-talk.

"Hey Bob, how are you?"

"Fine, you?"

"Great. How's the family?"

"Good."

"Hot today, huh?"

"Yes… yes it is… it is hot."

Formality, for all of its benefits, can be a big obstacle to authentic conversation. This is where discipleship-based small groups shine, sparkle, glow, explode if well done. Effective discipleship is, by nature, intimate and conversational. Therefore, an informal atmosphere that facilitates conversation within the small group makes these types of small groups hum.

SPIRITUAL CONVERSATIONS

In my personal small group's time of discussion, I made it my job to keep the ball moving, the conversation flowing. I'd do my best to draw out those who were more reserved and my equal best to, good-naturedly, contain those who tended to dominate the conversation. You WILL have both. I look for participation from all without giving the sense of controlling the dialogue; it's a subtle art, gained over time by those who pay attention to the need for it. Asking the right open ended questions is an important part of that art. People learn best when they are able to talk, so facilitating the conversation is paramount.

For my group, I wanted structure without formality, unity without uniformity and organic openness without a free-for-all. It's the facilitator's job to stay on topic, but be flexible enough to let the discussion develop naturally, and, indeed, Spiritually, in order to go where the group members need it to go and where the Holy Spirit wants it to go. There is a learning curve to becoming adept at this; it's vital, therefore, for future leaders to come up under seasoned leaders as part of their group and witness how groups function. Watch; do while watched; do and debrief; lead; train up others.

There is a huge spiritual work in a Discipleship based small group. Leaders need to be sensitive to this, to how God may be leading them, watching to see what He is doing among the group. This is the greatest part of these types of small groups. I have seen people change in conversation, seen God move in the conversation, seen God do a work in people as they share, as they air out their hearts, as they receive from others, hear God's Word. In this way, the leader should be Spirit led, Spirit sensitive, always alert to how the Spirit may be leading the conversation and leading the leader.

This is how we are GOing and making disciples within a group. This is where discipleship comes in. It comes with the discussion, with the lessons, and the questions surrounding the subject matter. It comes in when people are able to openly and safely talk about their issues, their doubts, their struggles. It comes with being a Spirit led example, because it comes in the watching. It comes in the accountability that a good small group provides.

I'm of the belief that in discipleship, people learn by watching the discipler. Disciples watch how leaders conduct themselves in various situations, how they field objections, handle disagreements, help people with needs, how they pray; they observe their temperaments and how they control their emotions. There are a lot of tests that come up for the leader in a group dynamic and people watch how leaders deal with each of them. More often than not, people learn more by what we do than what we say. It is a subtle danger. We are trying to win people to Christ, not win arguments.

CROSS-POLLINATION

In some small group models, "cross-talk" (group members talking to one another during the meetings), is discouraged. This censure makes sense in certain settings… like church services, or large groups. It helps to maintain order, silences potential bad advice, avoids rabbit trails, etc.

In our model, however, "cross-talk," what I preferred to think of as cross-pollination is encouraged, because I believe it has major benefits: 1. It exposes the real situations of the group members. 2. It has a cathartic value. 3. It maximizes the collective wisdom of the group. 4. It helps undiscovered leaders emerge 5. It provides an opportunity for every group member to participate in Jesus' commission to make disciples.

Disagreements and differing viewpoints, when respectfully discussed, are beneficial, if, in no other way, by exposing the practical and theological needs of the group. If someone in my group believes that God is a fuzzy squirrel, it helps me, as a leader, to know it. I want to know why they think God is a fuzzy squirrel; I want to know how they came to that conclusion; I want to know in what way their fuzzy squirrel theology affects their day-to-day life. It's easier to just tell people what to believe or how to live than it is to get into their lives, to find out what makes them tick. Rather than dictating truth, we want to lead people into a place of discovery.

We have to meet people where they are. Therefore, as group leaders, we needed to listen and assume nothing. We needed to know where people are coming from in their theological beliefs and disbeliefs in order to know how to properly and effectively guide, instruct and minister to them. Open conversations facilitate this entire process.

I loved seeing people helping one another, sharing from their own experiences, I didn't need to be the know-it-all, or have a tight reign of control on the group. We found that our leaders could maintain order and still allow for open conversation and if the advice one group member gave to another was off, the leader could give slight correction in the group, or after. These were great teaching opportunities I didn't want exchange for the comfort of control.

As it turned out, off putting advice was infrequent enough to validate the risk. What we experienced, on the whole, was older Christians helping younger Christians. The opportunity afforded older Christians a much-needed chance to contribute to the disciple-making process. We experienced younger Christians sharing with others who were struggling with similar issues, and even younger Christians encouraging the older, more mature Christians who needed it. It was exciting and genuinely spiritual. We witnessed God doing amazing things through cross-pollination and far be it from us to stop this from happening.

CRUCIAL CONVERSATIONS

We asked the question in an earlier chapter, *How do you respond when people disagree with you?* It's a powerful question. In the best selling book, *Critical Conversations,* the authors make the claim, "the root cause of many—if not most—human problems lies in how people behave when others disagree with them about high-stakes, emotional issues." They suggest that, "dramatic improvements in organizational performance were possible if people learned skills routinely practiced by those who have found a way to master these high-stakes, crucial moments." We agree, and will touch on some of these routinely practiced skills below.

When Britney and I were engaged, my dad gave me this advice: "You need a *system* to resolve your conflicts." My father is very a methodical guy. So, it was fitting advice coming from him, probably advice he learned from his own mistakes, but, at the time, I thought, *a system? Who does that? What does that even mean?* I didn't want to know, because I didn't want to treat my marriage as if it came with a set of instructions, or user manual, b.) When conflict arises, see diagram a. and follow steps 14-27. *Oh brother… can you even create a system like that?* Then, in our first year of marriage, my wife and I had some pretty heated conflicts, real doozies and I thought, *I think I need a system to resolve my conflicts.*

Dear old Dad was right; we needed a system. In the moment of disagreement, we all need the awareness and ability to dial back our emotions… *put down the lamp… think clearly, step away from the edge, breath, count to ten…. commuuuuuuuunicate.* Easier said than done right? In the heat of the battle, responding and communicating correctly can become like speaking a foreign language, or parsing verbs… excruciatingly hard for anyone but Dr. Sargent.

Having a system means that we are ready to handle conflict well; it means we have a contingency plan. It's vital in life, in marriage and in all of our relationships, especially in a discipleship relationship. When it comes to making disciples, there will always be disagreements. In today's Church climate, millenials and the de-churched, as we've learned, are highly sensitive to how we handle disagreements.

They say you shouldn't talk about politics or religion (some of my favorite topics of discussion) because they tend to engender the most conflict. So, in a way, Christians, as soul chasers and world-changers, are in the business of creating conflict. I think we do okay on that front. That being the case, we need to be better than your average bear at resolving conflict.

To help us with this, lets list some of the "system" steps from *Crucial Conversations:*[vi]

1. Find ways to get all relevant information in the open through dialogue.

2. Start with the heart, stay focused on what you really want.

3. Learn to look, notice when safety is at risk; be able to pull out to see what's happening to ourselves and to others during an argument.

4. Make it safe to talk about almost anything.

5. Don't shut down, stay in dialogue when you're angry, scared, or hurt.

6. Speak persuasively, not abrasively.

7. Listen when others blow up, or clam up.

8. Turn crucial conversations into action and results.

This is a good system to resolve conflict and we highly recommend this book to anybody, especially pastors or church leaders. For me, being brought up in the hot headed northeast; I find number three to be the hardest. Living in the south has surely softened my northern edges, but still this is a toughie. One of the most important qualities we can possess when it comes to resolving conflict, especially in a discipleship relationship is self-awareness—having the compassion in the moment not just to *be* right, but to respond and react right.

They are all great points, but, for our purpose, I'd like to explore number four. It plays a significant role small groups and one-on-one discipleship settings.

PLAYING IT SAFE

My wife and I love going to a good church-growth seminar. We've been to quite a few. Sometimes, a good seminar will bring in an influential motivational speaker from the world of business to share their techniques of team building within a corporation. One of the most recurring questions asked revolves around this question, *What makes an organization healthy?*

Frequent answer—*safety*.

By *safety*, we do not mean the physical safety of an office, or a church, but, rather a safe place for ideas, where open discussion and transparency are cultivated. When people feel free to speak their minds and hearts respectfully without sensing that they may suffer dire consequences, or judgment for it, then it's considered a *safe* place; that's a demarcation of health in an organization. Let's be clear, though, insane asylums have people speaking their minds all day and night, and have a safe place to do it in, that doesn't automatically make it a healthy environment. Even so, you can't have health without that freedom.

I read a meme once that said, "the next time you are afraid to share your idea because it may sound dumb, remember, once upon a time, someone sat in a meeting and said, 'Let's make a movie about tornados filled with sharks.'" People are risk adverse. To get the best ideas and most creative solutions, you need a *safe* environment. In order to create a *safe* environment, a culture has to be created where people are welcome to respectfully disagree, offer solutions, opinions and beliefs. *Safety* breeds health both in the corporate environment as well as a in the spiritual.

Creating a *safe* environment in a church means offering a place for people to find authentic community where they can have open relationships and honest dialogue without risking everything on a foible or controversial opinion.

While going to Bible College, I made the mistake of sharing one of Dr. Sargent's provocative interpretations about David and Goliath at a Bible study at my church. Get him to tell you about how David hit Goliath in the leg sometime, but be careful with whom you share it. I was laughed to scorn. It was as if I stood up and declared that Jesus wasn't God. I guess I should have seen it coming; some of those studies weren't exactly *safe* places to share controversial ideas.

Safety in small groups and in a one-on-one discipleship setting frees people to talk about almost anything without ruin or even contempt. It's the key to effective disciple-making. If you've ever benefitted from the *safety* of such a group, or suffered at the hands of an unsafe group, I'm sure you'll agree.

Though we don't believe in conforming our churches and message to the emotionalism of the de-churched, we do believe that some of their frustrations are legitimate and can be fruitfully addressed and eased, making them reachable. Let's interpret this common complaint of the de-churched, the feeling that they had to mindlessly conform without discussion to a system of beliefs before they would be accepted. What are they really saying? It's pretty simple—they want a *safe* place. I understand and can relate to this desire. It is legitimate; I want the same thing. People need a *safe* space. Healthy, conversational small groups and close one-on-one relationships meet this need.

My wife, Britney has quite a gift for making people feel *safe*, accepted and loved, almost immediately. I see her work this miracle all the time. We travel to a lot of places, meet many people, work with plenty of difficult musicians, insecure singers and domineering sound guys, navigate some pretty tough pastors and leaders. Britney can melt the coldest heart, sooth the most rumpled ego, tame the most savage sound guy. Give her anybody… I challenge you… the harder the better. It's one of the qualities that made me fall in love with her. It's definitely her spiritual gift, like spreading spiritual flowers. Her compassion and empathy is humbling to witness.

This is an important skill when making modern day disciples. We have to help people feel safe with us, accepted by us and loved by God through us.

I asked Britney if she would be willing to share some of her secrets with us here.

SPREADING FLOWERS

Britney:

My husband asked me, what goes on in your mind when you meet someone who's "stand off-ish" or withdrawn? How do you pull them out of their shell and bridge that gap relationally? This is a little uncomfortable to write about, because I'm no expert on the matter. I don't have a set system, but if I were to think about it, if someone is standoffish, or in someway closed, then I suppose that I try to identify their fear. I try to pay careful attention to both their verbal and non-verbal communication (the latter usually being the most telling). What are they afraid of, and what are they trying to protect?

We all have our social barriers that we put up when meeting new people. However, in my experience, if a person is overly hesitant to engage with or connect with others, it is almost always rooted in fear and insecurity. Often it's the fear of rejection. *"If they get to know who I really am and what I really struggle with, then they won't like or accept me… and I don't want to feel that hurt or shame."* Survival instincts kick in and walls go up to protect their heart from the possibility of future pain.

Other times, insecurity is founded in a fear of loss. In these cases, they may be trying to protect the things that make them feel most secure, like their status, position, power or influence. With this fear of loss, comes the reaction to protect. This is territorialism and it becomes the strongest when we are afraid of losing our identity or things that we believe define us.

In church, this type of territorialism can be demonstrated when worship leaders are resistant to sharing the platform with other musicians or singers for fear of being "out-shined," or when pastors won't to share the pulpit with other ministers due to insecurities of their own. *"I've been the best at* (fill in the blank) *for years; don't think for a second you're going to come in here and take that away from me!"*

We all struggle with fear and insecurity to varying degrees, and that's why I think it's easy to identify it in others. So once the fear is identified, how do we then help combat it so that a healthy relationship can be fostered? The Bible tells us it's love… *perfect love that casts out fear* (1 John 4:18). I think one of the greatest things we can do when trying to start a relationship with someone riddled with insecurity is to personify God's love by opening ourselves up, reaching out to them, making ourselves available and being as authentic as possible.

A former pastor of ours once said, "Don't take yourself too seriously… no one else does." Humor is always good, and finding a way to laugh at yourself, to "not take yourself too seriously," is advantageous and loosens people up. So be vulnerable; put yourself out there; ask questions; be open and humble; show people that you're genuinely interested in them; show people that you care. Don't overcomplicate it—be a friend!

I realize that not everybody's an extravert and that social skills come more naturally to some than to others, but regardless, everybody has the ability to be a good friend to someone. Proverbs 18:24 *"A man who has friends must himself be friendly."* Discipleship and friendship go hand in hand, and there isn't some secret formula. Just GO and be a friend—get busy *spreading those flowers!*

---

vi Crucial Conversations, Tools for Talking When the stakes are high. McGraw Hill (2012)

9

 UNITY VS. UNIFORMITY

John 16:31

Jesus answered them, "Do you now believe?"

Jonathan:

When I gave my life to the Lord, I had a real crisis. Since the age of 13, rock music had been my whole world. A decade of rock n' dreams was finally coming to fruition with my band. Jesus complicated things for me. I wanted to keep playing the venues that we had been—the bars and nightclubs… where the "sinners" were. I knew that as a Christian, the spirit and content of my music would change. I felt, however, that if I was going to be effective in reaching people for Christ, if I was going to GO and reach my community, then I couldn't do that by just playing music within the four walls of my small local church? It was a real challenge. I had a meeting with my pastor to discuss my ideas of continuing to play our music in the clubs.

We talked in his office for two hours. I shared my plan— the light of Christian music in a dark nightclub, evoking both witness and conversation. A little crazy? Overambitious for a young Christian? Maybe. But I was eager, optimistic and striving to act on faith. I wanted to reach people for the Lord and this made perfect sense to me.

Throughout our meeting in his small, wood paneled office, my pastor shot my ideas down like clay pigeons… *kablam…*

kablam! Oh, here comes another stupid idea… kablam! Oddly enough, when his target practice was over, I felt a little better, not resolved, but, at least, heard. He, however, felt like it was a big waste of his time. I remember him looking at his watch and saying, "That was two hours I wasted talking about this." *Ouch!*

During the following Sunday morning service, he spoke about our meeting to the congregation, saying, "I'll never talk to Cashman about music again. I wasted two hours of my time…" *Ouch again!* I was hurt. So hurt in fact that it's a miracle that I didn't get up and leave the church there and then.

I'm not trying to make my old pastor out to be a big bad guy. I'm not suggesting he didn't care about me, but what I am saying is that he didn't understand my struggle and didn't feel it personally beneficial to have talked so long with me about it. Instead, he felt like it was a big "waste of time" if I didn't kowtow. If I didn't immediately change my thinking, I was wasting his time. It may not have been a big deal to him, but it was an awful big deal to me at that time. Music was my life and I was confronting the potential death of my dreams, a little consideration would have gone a long way.

I was okay with my pastor not agreeing with me, but I needed him to hear me out, to understand my position, my dilemma. The challenge of maturity is that its ability to see the fleeting nature of youthful pains and struggles, the folly of many youthful aspirations tends to breed a detached contempt for those struggles when being suffered by the young. Just so, he saw my ideas as clay pigeons to be shot out of the air. He may have thought that I was just trying to stay in the club scene and perhaps his way of keeping me out of temptation and trouble was to shut the door on the conversation. He didn't take my struggle seriously and was frustrated that the conversation carried on so long. I was supposed to simply listen to his wisdom, drop my concerns and instantly embrace his vision for my life. He was a great pastor in a lot of ways, but it was obvious that in the area of music ministry, he was more interested in indoctrinating me than discipling me. I got over it, got through it and eventually found my way.

So why didn't I leave that Sunday morning after the, I'll-never-talk-to-Cashman-about-music-again sermon? I stayed because, and probably only because the Lord had me there and He had other people at that church who were speaking into my life as well. Sometimes it takes a village to raise a child and the mature Christians in that church were discipling me. They were there for me. They were people who understood what I was going through and who loved me enough to listen to my ideas, no matter how crazy they may have seemed... You know... crazy... like witnessing to my friends, like going where the sinners are, like using music as a tool for the gospel and not just as Christian worship or entertainment. What was I thinking?

Bottom line. Disciplers are going to have disagreements with those they seek to disciple. Consider their dilemmas and handle them well.

HOW DO YOU HANDLE DISAGREEMENT?

You don't need uniformity to have unity. Full uniformity is a daydream, a fairy tale; it can't happen, won't happen. Complete uniformity is actually unhealthy and unnatural; the very attempt to obtain it is oppressive and breaks the human spirit. It demands threat, compulsion, force and in extreme cases, violence. Because it can't be created, the illusion of it can't be sustained. Forced conformity usually stems from ignorance, insecurity and a sick need to control rather than influence, to overwhelm rather than convince. It is the tool of the wicked and the lazy. My pastor wasn't so much doing this; he wasn't forcing conformity, but the spirit of, *if you don't believe like me, than I have no time for you,* felt, at least passively, like I was being compelled to conform. He cared about me and that won the day, but in discipleship, we have to be aware and cautious of this compulsion to control and force uniformity.

Andrew's father-in-law once complained, "I raised my kids to think for themselves, I just never imagined that when they did they'd disagree with me." We don't have to believe exactly the same things to have healthy relationships, with friends, family, or even in the church; everyone is healthier for the challenges of diversity.

In a discipleship relationship, it is important to listen, to understand and to learn where people are coming from. Discipling is NOT just telling people what to do or what to believe, it's not dominating them, it's not becoming the opinion-destroyer for Jesus. Discipling is most effective when we facilitate people's discovery of divine truth from the divine Savior. It's sad that this even has to be stated here, but when we listen and are considerate of people's doubts and beliefs when they don't line up with our own, we are validating their natural God given rights as people. This is a position of strength rather than weakness. There is an old saying: People don't care what you know 'til they know that you care. Healthy, honest and authentic discussion demonstrates care. It is, however, a lot more work than being dictatorial or argumentative.

There is a really funny comic—a man sitting in front of his computer writing feverously. His wife calls from another room, "Honey, come to bed, I'm tired." He retorts, "I can't come right now, someone is wrong on the internet." Haven't you met this person? Can you see yourself as this person at times? I sure can in me. There's a propensity in most of us to correct, to enlighten others with our vision of reality, even on the most basic things. Just ask a Grammar-Natzi. Debate and discussion is good and healthy, but lurking always in the shadows around it is an unhealthy desire to set people straight. When this unhealthy inclination comes over into Christianity, it infiltrates our discipleship and can wreak havoc. We can almost believe that in some warped way that it is our Christian duty to set people straight and that setting people straight is our way of upholding the truth for Jesus. We have never seen good fruit in this. Reference the, God-hates-gays Westboro Baptists if you disagree. Though it may feel good to attempt to just set people straight, to tell people how they must conform, as followers of Christ, this is not our job. It is our duty to make disciples and this is infinitely more difficult as it takes a heart of love, understanding and care. Confrontation is inevitable, how we handle confrontation however is critical.

Andrew had a colleague many years ago whose entire approach to ministry was insulting, demanding, accusing and demeaning others. One day, when called to account by someone in authority for his unseemly and uncharitable behavior, he is reputed to have replied, "God has given me a ministry of confrontation." This authority figure, not to be outdone, said, "The only one in the Bible with a ministry of confrontation is Balaam's ass and if you want to minister like an ass you can do it elsewhere." Some people will reject Christ no matter how He's presented. Others, however, are driven away by the unseemly behavior of His servants. It cannot be overstated—people's right to differing views ought always to be validated. We should *never* belittle, scoff or ridicule any person's beliefs no matter how foreign to us they may be. We want to communicate well, but in order to be great communicators; we have to be great listeners and patient teachers.

In studying the de-churched, Packard and Hope found that the lack of authentic communication was one of the major factors driving people out of and, eventually away from the church. One of their respondents summarized this issue well, stating,

> I wasn't looking for agreement... I just
> wanted someone to talk to. Our old pastor never
> got angry or anything. He was civil. He kept me
> in church and could get me back. I mean, we

could even discuss evolution. But with the new pastor, it was all authority and hierarchy, and that was the final straw in getting us to leave. When we couldn't talk anymore, it just wasn't worth going.[vii]

Another respondent in the study said,

I had a chat with a pastor at a church that I was interested in attending, and I said, "I don't want to hear about what you believe; there will be plenty of time to talk about that later. I'm not interested in seeing if we agree, because I'm sure there will be disagreement. The only question I have for you is, How do you deal with people who disagree with you? How does you church handle that? Because really, for me, that's the most important thing.

I want to be in a place that welcomes disagreement. Not to disagree to be rude or nasty, but out of legitimate differences of opinion. Being able to express those differences openly is a more authentic experience of faith to me. I think my biggest fear is that I'm going to get into another situation where I'm going to be the one asking questions, and I'm going to be shuffled out the door again. And I don't want that. I have to be able to ask questions. It's how I learn."[viii]

Did you catch what he said? "The only question I have for you is, *How do you deal with people who disagree with you?*" That's quite a question isn't it? We would do well to ask ourselves, "How do *I* deal with people who disagree with me?" This question summarizes a large part of the wide-scale aversion that we are seeing in people these days to the Church.

I take the philosophy that good leadership, good discipleship doesn't overwhelm people, doesn't intimidate them, dictate to them, bully them, treat them like bad children that wrote on the wall with crayons. We don't win people to Christ by force. Unlike many other religions, neither Christianity nor Judaism have traditionally sought to advance themselves at the tip of a sword (though there have been exceptions among some misguided followers). Jews and Christians have traditionally favored wooing, winning, appealing, guiding. Beliefs that are embraced through the changing of the heart cannot be advanced through the overwhelming of the will. Our job as disciplers, as GOers isn't to dictate to people what they must think, or what they need to believe, our job is to influence, to teach, to train, to encourage… anything else may boarder on manipulation.

We are healthier if we navigate disagreement well than if we never had disagreement to begin with. "As iron sharpens iron, so one man sharpens another" (Prov 27:17 NASB). Rather than being a parrot, we ought to know why we believe what we believe. Often disagreements force us to articulate those beliefs, help us to think on our feet, give us reason to study, opportunity to demonstrate why we believe what we do, expanding our thinking and put our preconceived notions and biases to the test.

One of the most important moments of developmental crisis in Andrew's life came when a prostitute in New York City schooled him on his own shallow understanding of the gospel he was preaching through a Four Spiritual Laws track. When it became obvious that he could not answer a handful of penetrating questions about the nature of Christ's sacrifice and what it meant for her practically, she scolded him for such a bold proclamation of a message that he himself did not adequately understand. After a short bout with tears, it set him on the course to becoming a biblical theologian.

CORE BELIEFS & PERIPHERAL INTERPRETATIONS

In discipleship, we are not striving for uniformity of belief on all issues and doctrines, but we are training Christian disciples and that entails certain commitments.

Imagine two circles, a small inner and a larger outer. The inner circle contains what we would call *core beliefs*, a biblical worldview, historically defined doctrines of God and man, Christ and gospel, a commitment to biblical inspiration, defense of clearly established biblical moral standards, etc. These would be beliefs we wouldn't change, doctrines we would teach and defend, giving the biblical and historical what and why of the Christian faith.

The outer circle would be what we would consider, *peripheral interpretations*, wisdom choices. These are points that can be and are reasonably debated, even from Scripture. It is important, therefore, that we allow charity and a desire for unity to dominate when we collide over these issues.

Most will defend the church's hope in Christ's 2nd coming (*a core belief*), divide from each other over eschatological timelines? Few would defend drunkenness, but should we disassociate from casual consumers? Baptism and communion are core Church practice. but should we ostracize people, or divide over sprinkling vs. immersion, or the frequency and process of the Lord's supper? What about movies, music, dancing, playing cards, television, modesty standards?

Knowing what is *core* and what is *peripheral* will help you to keep the main thing the main thing. Spend quality time on *core* issues with people and the *peripherals* won't matter as much. One of Andrew's professors once quipped, "There is no such thing as THE Christian life, there are simply Christians living their lives… some wisely, some foolishly, most a solid mix of the two."

It is vital that we distinguish our *core* beliefs from *peripheral* issues. Blurring the lines can be reckless. If we take *peripheral* issues and make them *core*, we dance on the edge of legalism; we end up creating a club culture, where you're either in or out based on exacting doctrinal commitments, and highly specific behaviors that are more likely a list of things you don't do rather than things you do do. Just so, when we take *core* beliefs and make them *peripheral*, we run the risk of abolishing absolute God-given biblical standards and truth and disconnecting ourselves from historical Christianity.

By way of a recent example, consider the colossal challenge by the LGBT community to the church's core beliefs regarding human sexuality and gender. Some believe that "Male and Female He made them" (Genesis 1:27) is flexible, peripheral to Christian doctrine and to the church's message. They think Leviticus 18:22 "You shall not lie with a male as with a woman; it is an abomination" is skirtable for any number of rationalizations and unimportant in light of the supposed pulse of Jesus' superseding message of love and acceptance. Can you embrace and defend what Paul called "shameful," "vile passions," redefine biblical marriage, and openly embrace men as women and women as men without forsaking the very essence of Christianity? Can you patiently guide a willing disciple through the process of discovering a biblical worldview?

DON'T BE A KNOW-IT-ALL

What our goals ought to be in making disciples is not to create robotic clones that believe every jot and tittle of what *we* believe, but rather to create relationships that are open, honest and truth seeking. God is big and we don't know everything, but there is a temptation to carry ourselves as if we do, because we think we should. This can be damaging when done with core beliefs, but even more so when it comes to the peripherals. A *know-it-all* approach shuts the door to people who may need to think out loud about spiritual issues, who desire to wrangle with truth rather than being indoctrinated. Canned responses, cheap answers and dismissive retorts demonstrates ignorance and careless and will cut short your influence faster than almost anything you could do.

I didn't adopt beliefs about God and Scripture because someone told me I needed to believe this way or that. Rather, in my discipleship relationships, I argued; I debated; I gave alternate viewpoints. I grew in my theology based on patient challenge and solid argument that drove me to deeper study, impassioned prayer, dependence on the Holy Spirit, and hard won life experiences. It's been a journey for me and, as a discipler, I try to keep in mind that others are on their own journey as well. It can be difficult to witness people to go through their own process with God. We often feel obligated to play God in the lives of disciples. There can even be a sense of guilt that by saying, "I don't know," or by hearing differing viewpoints, we will lessen our influence and let God down by allowing God to lose "the debate," diminishing both their faith and God's work in their life. Nothing could be further from the truth.

Let's look at Jesus. He taught openly and invited questions. The people that He shuts down and rebukes regularly are the *know-it-all* religious folks, the Pharisees, Sadducees and scribes;

those who are unteachable, high-minded and prideful. If we look at how He taught, we see that Jesus taught with authority, but He wasn't an overzealous salesman. He was okay with taking open aired questions. He was okay with doubt and wasn't angry at struggling disbelief. He gave answers that drew people out, caused them to think. He was patient, even with His disciples, allowing them to discover Him as Christ. Remember, they weren't good Christian boys when He called them. He allowed them to follow Him, doubts and all, then they believed; too often we say believe and then you can follow. We need to allow time for the discipleship process to work and for faith to grow.

It was on Jesus' last night with His disciples, after one of His final conversations about how He would be leaving them that some of His disciples finally got it and confessed their belief in Him. Jesus answered, "Do you *now* believe? (John 16:31) He's like, *seriously, now you believe? After all this time, after all that you've seen me do, heard me teach… seriously, now you believe? The miracles, the healings, the feeding thousands, the walking on the water thing, that didn't do it for ya?*

What's important to note here is that the whole time the twelve were with Him, Jesus never forced them to the point where they had to believe or leave. In fact, He lived with measures of their unbelief for a long while; though often frustrated, He embraced them, little faith, doubts and all, even to the very end.

The famous, "Doubting Thomas," didn't believe until after the crucifixion and resurrection. He wouldn't believe that Christ had been raised from the dead, despite all that Jesus foretold about His coming resurrection, despite the eyewitness accounts of his friends. It wasn't 'til He saw the risen Christ; saw the wounds in His hands and side that he *finally* believed. Jesus was patient with people. We should be too.

Jesus' example demonstrates to us that if we are to be effective disciple-makers, then we have to accept where people are in their discipleship process, so long as it IS a process. *Know-it-alls*, demand immediate belief, pushing growing people away. The *know-it-all* attitude communicates pride, close mindedness, insecurity and it shuts the door on those wrestling their way to faith.

Jesus said, "GO make disciples, teaching them all the things that I commanded you," not, "GO make robotic, unthinking clones, commanding them to obey without understanding." Listen; guide; nudge; call; teach; love; cheer; pray; encourage; lead; feed; seed; weed; challenge and correct patiently, making disciple-making-disciples of all nations.

[vii] Josh Packard Ph.D. & Ashleigh Hope, Church Refugees, Loveland: Group Publishing (2015), P.21-36

[viii] Josh Packard Ph.D. & Ashleigh Hope, Church Refugees, Loveland: Group Publishing (2015), P.21-36

10

° GOOD INTENSIONS °

Romans 12:1

I beseech you therefore, brethren, by the mercies of God, that you present your bodies a living sacrifice, holy, acceptable to God, which is your reasonable service.

Ephesians 5:8-10

For you were once darkness, but now you are light in the Lord. Walk as children of light (for the fruit of the Spirit is in all goodness, righteousness, and truth), finding out what is acceptable to the Lord.

2 Corinthians 5:9

Therefore we make it our aim, whether present or absent, to be well pleasing to Him.

Philippians 3:13

I do not count myself to have apprehended; but one thing I do, forgetting those things which are behind and reaching forward to those things which are ahead.

Jonathan:

My wife, Britney and I are from New England… *how-ah-ya?!* That's where we met and fell in love. We moved (separately) to Nashville, TN… *how-y'all-doin'?!* …in hopes of furthering our music ministry. We were engaged within our first year of living there. During the time of our engagement, I was working hard to get us established. It was 2005-2006, and the real estate market was cooking hot. I went to real estate school, got my license and became an agent. I started making good money, bought a big house with a big pool, and an even bigger mortgage. We were soon married and moved into the new house. We were both working and though we were making decent money, we had a hard time keeping up with the other big bills, car loan, credit cards, utilities, not to mention the hefty fees, dues and other costs of being a real estate agent. I started to build a real estate team and was doing pretty good for a newer agent. Things went okay our first year, we had a nice house, two nice cars, a pool, good friends… but there was something amiss. We were going to a predominant church in the area that taught us that the kind of affluent lifestyle we were living was what God wanted for us, but, still something seemed off. We played on the worship team and served in the young adult ministry, but, for the most part the ministry that God had given to us was stagnant.

At the time, I had been reading the journals of John Wesley, Charles Wesley and George Whitfield. Each mentioned a recently published book that had heavily influenced their faith—William Law's, *A Serious Call to the Devout and Holy Life,* 1729. The title itself was enough to scare some curiosity into me. Then I thought, *wait I think I actually have that book*. Early in my Christian walk, I prayed for wisdom and God answered by having random people give me books, lots of book, sometimes boxes of books, a supernatural endowment would have been a lot less work, but I asked for it. Soon, I had built up a nice little library and, sure enough, that book was on my shelf. It was as big as you'd expect a book with that daunting of a title to be. About the size of the New York City telephone directory (an ancient book once used to catalogue phone numbers). I took it down *A Serious Call to a Devout and Holy Life* and started reading it as part of my morning devotions. As I read, I would get increasingly frustrated with Mr. Bill Law. "This guy is so legalistic!" I'd blurt. Perhaps he was, but I couldn't put it down. The book was a plea for reform, a call to real devotion, but his expectations seemed impossible to live by. On the other hand, I had to admit that for everyone other than William Law himself, I suppose, pure devotion is impossible. The real problem I was having was that he made too much painful sense. For all of my grievances with his perfectionism, I couldn't escape his logic. It had me in a headlock.

One of the topics he spoke of most was intentionality. He defines sincere and godly intention as, "intending to please God in all the actions of your life," regarding it as, "the happiest and best thing in the world."[ix] That's pretty straightforward. I wondered if pleasing God was that high on my list. Could I say that I considered God's pleasure in all my actions the happiest and best thing in the world? I doubted it. He went on to say::

> "It was this general *intention* that made the primitive Christians such eminent instances of piety, and made the goodly fellowship of the saints, and all the glorious army of martyrs and confessors. And if you will here stop, and ask yourselves, why you are not as pious as the primitive Christians were, your own heart will tell you, that it is neither through ignorance nor inability, but purely because you never thoroughly intended it." [x]

Ouch! That old Englishman chaffed my goodly hide. Unfortunately, I knew exactly what he meant by this kind of intention. He wasn't talking about *the road to hell is paved with good intentions* kind of intentions, but, rather, a sincere motivation of the heart, an absolute intention that drives us to do what we do, to be who we are, to achieve the goal, run the race, win the prize, and forgo all else. This idea of Godly intention, of

purposefully intending to please God in all my actions without fail, vacation, sick days, or time off for bad behavior as the greatest thing in life began to dominate my thinking. I kept seeing this concept in my Bible readings. Jesus, in summing up the Law and the Prophets said, "You shall love the LORD your God with all your heart, with all your soul, and with all your mind.' This is *the* first and great commandment.
And *the* second *is* like it: 'You shall love your neighbor as yourself" (Matthew 22:37-39). Sounds like an aggressive, intentional commitment to please God me. He criticized Pharisees and Sadducees saying that they, "Loved the approval of men rather than the approval of God." (John 12:43) The Apostle Paul described intentional God pleasing this way:

> *No soldier gets entangled in civilian pursuits, since his aim is to please the one who enlisted him. An athlete is not crowned unless he competes according to the rules. It is the hard-working farmer who ought to have the first share of the crops. Think over what I say, for the Lord will give you understanding in everything.* (2 Timothy 2:4-7) ESV

Paul's right. This concept of our own intentionality ought to be thought over, mulled over and over and over and over, asking ourselves weather we intend to please God in our actions and weather we consider pleasing God as the happiest and best thing in the world? I became entranced by the possibilities of a life so lived.

CALL IN HELP

I would like to share a portion of William Law's book that dramatically challenged and changed Britney's and my life from that day to this. It is a story that convicted me to a point of submission. This story stoked a fire within us, changing the entire course of our lives. It is a story of a man on his deathbed, speaking to a few close friends. It is a long story, but I'll give you a Reader's Digest version of it. William Law here introduces us to a man named Penitens:

> Penitens was a busy, notable tradesman, and very prosperous in his dealings, but died in the thirty-fifth year of his age. A little before his death, when the doctors had given him over, some of his neighbors came one evening to see him, at which time he spake thus to them.

> "I see, my friends, the tender concern you have for me, by the grief that appears in your countenances, and I know the thoughts that you have now about me. You think how melancholy a case it is, to see so young a man, and in such flourishing business, delivered up to death. And perhaps, had I visited any of you in my condition, I should have had the same thoughts of you.

> But now, my friends, my thoughts are no more like your thoughts than my condition is like yours. It is no trouble to me now to think, that I am to die young, or before I have raised an estate. These things are now sunk into such mere nothings, that I have no name little enough to call them by. For if in a few days or hours, I am to leave this carcass to be buried in the earth, and to find myself either forever happy in the favor of God, or eternally separated from all light and peace, can any words sufficiently express the littleness of everything else?

> Is there any dream like the dream of life, which amuses us with the neglect and disregard of these things? Is there any folly like the folly of our manly state, which is too wise and busy, to be at leisure for these reflections? When we consider

death as a misery, we only think of it as a miserable separation from the enjoyments of this life. We seldom mourn over an old man that dies rich, but we lament the young, that are taken away in the progress of their fortune. You yourselves look upon me with pity, not that I am going unprepared to meet the Judge of quick and dead, but that I am to leave a prosperous trade in the flower of my life.

For what is there miserable, or dreadful in death, but the consequences of it? When a man is dead, what does anything signify to him, but the state he is then in? ...The greatness of those things which follow death makes all that goes before it sink into nothing. Now that judgment is the next thing that I look for, and everlasting happiness or misery is come so near me, all the enjoyments and prosperities of life seem as vain and insignificant, and to have no more to do with my happiness, than the clothes that I wore before I could speak.

But, my friends, how am I surprised that I have not always had these thoughts? What a strange thing is it, that a little health, or the poor business of a shop, should keep us so senseless of these great things, that are coming so fast upon us!

Had I now a thousand worlds, I would give them all for one year more, that I might present unto God one year of such devotion and good works, as I never before so much as *intended*.

You, perhaps, when you consider that I have lived free from scandal and debauchery, and in the communion of the Church, wonder to see me so full of remorse and self-condemnation at the approach of death. But, alas! what a poor thing is it, to have lived only free from murder, theft, and adultery, which is all that I can say of myself.

It is true, I have lived in the communion of the Church, and generally frequented its worship and service on Sundays, when I was neither too idle, or not otherwise disposed of by my business and pleasures. …But the thing that now surprises me above all wonders is this, that I never had so much as a *general intention* of living up to the piety of the Gospel.

In the business of life I have used prudence and reflection. I have done everything by rules and methods. I have been glad to converse with men of experience and judgment, to find out the reasons why some fail and others succeed in any business. I have taken no step in trade but with great care and caution, considering every advantage or danger that attended it. I have always had my eye upon the main end of business, and have studied all the ways and means of being a gainer by all that I undertook. But what is the reason that I have brought none of these tempers to religion? What is the reason that I, who have so often talked of the necessity of rules, and methods, and diligence, in worldly business, have all this while never once thought of any rules, or methods, or managements, to carry me on in a life of piety?

Do you think anything can astonish and confound a dying man like this? What pain do you think a man must feel, when his conscience lays all this folly to his charge, when it shall show him how regular, exact, and wise he has been in small matters, that are passed away like a dream, and how stupid and senseless he has lived, without any reflection, without any rules, in things of such eternal moment, as no heart can sufficiently conceive them?

Had I only my frailties and imperfections to lament at this time, I should lie here humbly trusting in the mercies of God. But, alas! How can I call a general disregard, and a thorough neglect of all religious improvement, a frailty or imperfection, when it was as much in my power to have been exact, and careful, and diligent in a course of piety, as in the business of my trade?

I could have called in as many helps, have practiced as many rules, and been taught as many certain methods of holy living, as of thriving in my shop, had I but so *intended,* and desired it. Oh, my friends! a careless life, unconcerned and unattentive to the duties of religion, is so without all excuse, so unworthy of the mercy of God, such a shame to the sense and reason of our minds, that I can hardly conceive a greater punishment, than for a man to be thrown into the state that I am in, to reflect upon it."

Penitens was here going on, but had his mouth stopped by a convulsion, which never suffered him to speak any more. He lay convulsed about twelve hours, and then gave up the ghost.

Now if every reader would imagine this Penitens to have been some particular acquaintance or relation of his, and fancy that he saw and heard all that is here described; that he stood by his bedside when his poor friend lay in

such distress and agony, lamenting the folly of his
past life, it would, in all probability, teach him
such wisdom as never entered into his heart
before. …This therefore being so useful a
meditation, I shall here leave the reader, as I
hope, seriously engaged in it. (*sic*)

Penitens' ghost haunted me. I imagined what my thoughts
would have been had I been on of the firiends who stood by his
deathbed listening to the impact of eternity's siren call on his
soul. The line that stuck out to me the most was, "I could have
called in as many helps." That line, more than any other,
haunted me day after day. I went through a range of inner
opinions, tried to rationalize, to justify my lifestyle, but in the
end, I realized my trouble… I was living Penitens' life.

Like Penitens, I was a careful and disciplined investor in my
business. I was "calling in help," hiring people to my real estate
team, fulfilling my financial dreams, and it was this that got me
out of bed in the morning, what I was living for. A person can
be a success in business and still be in God's will, but I wasn't. I
wasn't throwing God over, exactly, but I was sacrificing an
eternal, heavenly reward for material success. I was devoting my
time, talent and energy to building a prosperous work, while
neglecting kingdom work, and the call of God. We were called
to something else.[xi]

GET UP AND GO

At first, I tried to pass off my feelings of conviction as a
manipulative guilt trip. I sat one night with Britney while we
soaked our legs in our pool in Nashville, and started sharing
with her all the thoughts that this book has spurred. I remember
asking her, "Do you think it's wrong for us to have all of this?"
The conclusion? God didn't bring us to Nashville so we could
sell real estate and accumulate lots of stuff; He called us to His

work, to tend His fields, to reap His harvest for His Kingdom. We had somehow forgotten this. We'd gone from being ministers and musicians who worked to pay the bills to being workers who played a little music and did a little ministry. Whatever God may have called others to, deep down, we knew this wasn't right for us. We weren't intentionally fulfilling His mission, and certainly not fulfilling His Great Commission to GO make disciples. He wanted more of us. So, thanks to William Law, I guess we had both become friends at Penitens' deathbed.

Penitens, in going through his deathbed "I could haves," was getting my wife and I to do the same. We started asking ourselves what more we could do for the kingdom? There was a lot. We started by selling our house and moving into a smaller apartment with a smaller monthly payment. We sold off a bunch of stuff we didn't need and downsized our whole lives. We had a conversation with the leaders of the prosperity church we were attending about our new convictions and were shown the door.

It was then, that the inspiration came to remake the musical about the Christ's Passion Week that I had written when I was young in the Lord. We started an editing/rewriting process that spanned over a year. When the musical was originally written, I called it, *King of All Kings;* we renamed it, *SAVIOR*. Upon completion, a friend introduced us to a great producer in Nashville and we started the recording process.

He called in some of the best talent we had ever seen or heard. Gifted, brilliant musicians, composers and singers came around the project. For two years, we felt like we were witnessing a miracle. From the attention to detail in the charting, to the level of brilliance in their playing and singing, to the quality of the recording, the musical came to life in ways I could never imagined. In the end, we had the double CD, with 90 minutes worth of music capturing the moods and the emotions of the Passion Week in 40 songs.

We were witnessing firsthand what it was like to "call in helps" for the work of the kingdom. God was in it; He was blessing it, and we were walking on air. During that same two years studio, Britney was inspired to write a worship album, which we developed and recorded there in the same studio with the same Godsend talent.

We grew leaps and bounds in that time. Challenged and inspired by the talent and hearts of the help God brought us, we grew. We became better writers, better players, better singers; we learned how to efficiently work in the studio, how to work professionally, to treat what God had given us with care, attention and *intention*.

Soon we had a manager and developed the SAVIOR live event. This would mean calling in a whole new set of helps. We called in video people to help with the multimedia show, called in a team of musicians for the live performance. We had success performing the musical in Nashville, then got ourselves packed up again and ready to hit the road when the phone rang. My mom was sick with cancer. It was stage 3b lung cancer. We were shocked and faced with a choice—continue touring, or move to Florida to be with my mom. We moved to Florida.

I took a position as Worship and Arts Director at a predominant church in Orlando and was able help my brother take care of my mom. During this time we developed SAVIOR even further. I started writing a 40 Day devotional around the 40 songs of the musical. I took each Biblical event that was represented in song and wrote a sort of commentary-apologetic-evangelistic devotional on it. When it was done… I didn't like it. Well, that's not exactly true… I hated it. You know your book is bad when even you don't want to read it… and I didn't. It read like a portion of Barnes Notes, or some other drabby commentary that sits on the shelf collecting dust along with its 20 other companions only to be pulled off for the occasional reference—fine for Barnes, not so good for a devotional. So I decided to add my personal story. I thought I'd relate to the lessons in the drabby commentary with my own testimony. It was much better, but now I had another problem—it was far too long. I had to call in help once more.

I thought of one of my favorite Bible School professors, Dr. Andrew Sargent, and sought him out. I asked if he'd be interested in helping me edit down my phone book of a devotional to some sort of normal size and semblance. He agreed. We've been writing together ever since.

While we finished editing the SAVIOR devotional, I took the position as Small Group Pastor at the church to go along with the worship leading. This opened the door to developing the devotional, now called, *40 Days with the SAVIOR,* into a small group curriculum. It seemed we were writing in a lab, so I took some of the church small groups through the chapters of the devotional, used the chapter questions for our small group discussions and took note of how the conversations naturally flowed. This caused a whole new editing process and also inspired Andrew and I to develop the *40 Days With the SAVIOR Leadership Guide.*

The Leadership Guide was written to develop small group leaders navigate in general and to help them navigate the conversations and avoid pitfalls specific to our devotional… most of which we discovered the hard way, by actually using the book in various small group settings.

While all this was happening the SAVIOR live event was continuing to take shape. Our church sat 5300, had a great platform for huge events like this, and provided all the technical advantages needed for a grand spectacle. This brought in a whole new slew of helps from media, to sound, acting, administration, directing, and even more musicians and singers. The results were humbling in many ways.

The goal with the musical was to engage our community, present the gospel with the production and make a call of salvation. We wanted to encourage those who came to Christ to get integrated into a discipleship small group setting, to take a 40-day challenge, to go 40 days with the SAVIOR. We wanted to get a book and CDs into their hands to guide them on that journey, and to connect them with Christian disciplers.

When my mom passed four years later, my wife and I felt called to travel full time. That first year of road ministry, we got a call from the largest Spanish church in Orlando to do the musical in Spanish… which neither my wife nor I speak. The church had a studio and they were willing to both translate the musical and re-record the vocals over the tracks that we originally recorded in Nashville. We then "called in help" with the translation of the *40 Days With the SAVIOR* devotional. The results—SALVADOR and *40 Dias Con El SALVADOR*. We performed it that Easter for 7000 to 8000 people, both in Spanish and in English. That day we witnessed the greatest altar call of our lives, over 400 people came forward to receive Christ.

…All from asking this question of intention regularly.

So, I'll ask it here of you as well. If you are going to be intentional about the Great Commission in you life, then ask yourself—*what is the highest and best use of your time talent and energy for the kingdom of God?* We all have our giftings, our callings, our talents, maybe yours is making money for the Kingdom, but we all share in this same mission—to make disciples. There is no happier purpose in life than to please God, and nothing pleases God like a life that is intentional in building His Kingdom, and nothing builds His Kingdom better than being intentional about making disciple-making disciples. Therefore, whatever you do with the investment of your time, talent and energy, let it be motivated by an *intention* to GO and make disciples.

You may be overwhelmed with the idea. Let me encourage you— we can achieve more together than we could ever do alone. Call in help!

You may be afraid of what your life will look like infused with divine *intention*, what it will be if dedicated to making disciples. Let me encourage you—Have this *intention* in your heart of making disciples, of fulfilling that Great Commission in your life, and the results will amaze you.

---

ix William Law, A Serious Call to a Devout and Holy Life, London: Paulist Press (1729) "Intentions" Pg. 69-74

x William Law, A Serious Call to a Devout and Holy Life, London: Paulist Press (1729) "Intentions" Pg. 69-74

xi William Law, A Serious Call to a Devout and Holy Life, London: Paulist Press (1729) "Intentions" Pg. 69-74

11

COUNT THE COST

Luke 14:28

"Which of you, intending to build a tower, does not sit down first and count the cost, whether he has enough to finish it?"

Jonathan:

Britney and I have traveled to hundreds of churches across America, singing and speaking on the importance of the Great Commission. The topic of disciple-making has been the burden of our hearts for many years, and we try, wherever we go to encourage people to make disciples… to start somewhere with someone. The responses we get are interestingly similar. People feel unqualified, disqualified, inept or incompetent to make disciples for any number of reasons. Most of these are self-inflicted disqualifications. It could be laziness, or selfishness looking for an excuse, or even lies of the enemy that have buried themselves in the mind and hearts of good people, but whichever it is, it's false and self-defeating. This is one of the main reasons we wrote this book—to help people to overcome these feelings of inadequacy and mental stumbling blocks that keep them from obeying this last great commandment from our Lord Jesus Christ.

Let's start off by stating the obvious; none of us are truly qualified to make disciples.

Even so, listen to what the Apostle Paul says about this:

> *To those who are called, both Jews and Greeks, Christ, the power of God and the wisdom of God. For the*

foolishness of God is wiser than men, and the weakness of God is stronger than men.

For consider your calling, brothers: not many of you were wise according to worldly standards, not many were powerful, not many were of noble birth. But God chose what is foolish in the world to shame the wise; God chose what is weak in the world to shame the strong; God chose what is low and despised in the world, even things that are not, to bring to nothing things that are, so that no human being might boast in the presence of God. And because of Him you are in Christ Jesus, who became to us wisdom from God, righteousness and sanctification and redemption, so that, as it is written, "Let the one who boasts, boast in the Lord."
(1 Corinthians 1:24-31 ESV)

God chooses the foolish, the weak, the low, the despised... this is the power of God! There is no inadequacy too great for God, He's not looking for perfect people, He's looking for willing and passionate people. Christ has changed our hearts, done a work in our lives and we do our very best to live by His Word and His Spirit and allow ourselves the opportunity to let God use us. At some point we have to trust God with our inadequacies and allow His Spirit to work through our brokenness.

Jesus chose twelve ordinary men to be His disciples. These men were as unqualified as they come, but they did possess willingness to follow and a passion for Christ. Teaching passion is like teaching someone to be hungry. We can motivate, encourage, train and educate, but without passion, these things falter. Without fuel, even a Rolls Royce goes nowhere. We have to be willing to allow ourselves to be moved, to allow God to light up our spirits. Sooner or later we have to say, "Yes Lord, You can use me... I will GO!"

YOUR FEAR TO GO

Britney:

This is a *safe* place, and so it is okay to admit that when it comes to GOing and making disciples, that we all struggle with some form of fear and insecurity. I know I do! It's called being human.

When I was a teenager and a new follower of Christ, I battled with feelings of inadequacy. I loved spending hours alone at the piano writing, singing and pouring out my heart in worship to the Lord. It was my way of expressing my love for Him and gratitude for all He'd done in my life. It was pure honest, and private… very private. It was certainly not something I felt comfortable sharing with the general public.

This went on for a while, but I began sensing the prompting of the Holy Spirit to begin stepping out and accepting opportunities to share this gift of music with others. I was petrified. Being the reserved, shy girl that I was at that time, a girl who cared *way* too much about what others thought of her… this call to "GO!" (even if it was just into my little community) was absolutely, knee-knockingly terrifying!

I immediately began recounting all the people in my life that were far more talented and qualified than I was. I reminded the Lord of other girls, even girls in my own class, that were far better singers than I was, and of the friends I had who were better pianists and songwriters than I was. I began seeing the faces of my peers and feeling the weight of their judgmental stares and the immense humiliation that I was sure would follow, until thankfully God stopped me mid-panic attack.

I'm not one of those crazy Christians who professes to casually hear from God about what breakfast cereal to eat, or which shampoo to buy… but I really believe I heard from God that day. It wasn't an audible voice from heaven, but it might as well have been. I clearly heard Him interrupt my self-deprecating thought process and tell me, "By comparing yourself to everyone else, you're making it all about you… and I want it to be all about me." *Ouch!*

That truth stung for sure, but it is a truth that has stuck with me. I was *disqualifying* myself from ministry, and God wouldn't let me. Afterwards, when presented with opportunities to share music at my school, or help lead worship at my church, I took them. Was I nervous? Absolutely! I was so nervous that you could see my knees knocking all the way from the back of the sanctuary. I pressed through it though, and every time I would start to worry about what others were thinking about me, I would close my eyes and remind myself, *Britney, it's not about you; it's about Him… it's not about you; it's about Him.* Slowly, but surely, my heart began to express itself freely, as if I was singing alone to Him in my living room again. I began glorifying God with all my heart, all my voice, all my ability and strength… regardless of what I feared others would think of me, because He was worthy, and that's all that mattered.

Even now, especially now with all of the great talented worship leaders that are out there, in the deep artist pool in which I find myself swimming. I could have all the more reason to fear and feel inadequate. When I hear that voice of comparison trying to discourage me, trying to disqualify me, I still have to remind myself—*It's not about m; it's about Him.*

Theodore Roosevelt once said, "Comparison is the thief of joy." I agree, I'd go one step further and say that comparison is the enemy of the work of God. The Apostle Paul says, "For we dare not class ourselves or compare ourselves with those who commend themselves. But they, measuring themselves by themselves, and comparing themselves among themselves, are not wise" (2 Corinthians 10:12). Not wise… that's a nice way of saying—*It's stupid.* Comparison can become The Great Self-disqualifier when it comes to fulfilling the call of God on our lives. Rather than comparing or competing with each other, we should be celebrating one another, encouraging one another… GOing with one another.

DISQUALIFIERS

Jonathan:

Good Christian people can often get the idea that the Church is a discipleship factory and the pastor is the CEO and therefore it's solely the pastor's job to make disciples. Isn't that right? Carpenters build things, plumbers plumb and ministers… well, they minister. The Bible tells us, however, that the pastor is to equip the saints for the work of the ministry (Ephesians 4:12). So the pastor is the equipper and we are the ministers.

People often say to me, "I don't feel like I know enough to disciple someone." Ignorance is a legitimate concern. Many, however, have been in the Lord for many years. How long were they intending on making this an excuse? Are they going to do anything to change this? How will they know when they know enough? While we are at it, who told them that this disqualified them?

David and Shelby, my guitar player and his wife, were only three months in the Lord when they discipled me. Three months! So to this feeling of inadequacy, I say, you don't have to know everything, you just have to stay a few lessons ahead. That's what David and Shelby did, they just shared what they knew and when they weren't sure of something, or if I gave them a stumper, they weren't afraid to say, "I don't know." The thing is, however, they were constantly being challenged by the discipleship relationship to learn. It gave them a powerful impetus to grow. This is huge! Discipleship changes the mentor, not just the mentee. There are some lessons you only learn by teaching. We often learn best on a need to know basis and there is no greater need to know than when you are discipling someone.

Past failure cripples many would-be mentors before they start. People who have messed up in their Christian walk, have had a moral failure, a falling away of some sort, often feel that they are now unfit to disciple someone else. It makes them feel like a hypocrite, How can I be an example to anyone when I've messed up so badly? This argument is built on a false premises. It assumes that perfection, or near perfection, is a prerequisite for being a Christian mentor, when the most significant components in a successful Christian mentorship relationship are being available, committed, knowledgeable and authentic. Sometimes great disciple-makers are those who have a testimony of victory over failure, those who know the stakes, who understand the importance of accountability and being there for someone.

Idle hands are often the devil's tools and idle minds his workshop. While some failures need close attention and should keep them from certain ministry for a time, or for good, we can be too hasty to disqualify others and ourselves based on a slip in their Christian walk. Rather than helping them get up and carry on, we often tell them, *sit down, do nothing*. Great discernment is needed in these delicate matters, but I tend to want people to get back in the fight before they lose their purpose.

When one of my guys would mess up, I'd do my best to throw them right back into ministry, get them to share at the small group, to lead in prayer, to facilitate the conversation… anything to get them back on the horse, to help them realize their purpose again.

Another disqualifier we hear is, *I'm not ready to make that kind of commitment to people*. This is the most honest so far. It is also the hardest to overcome. How do you get someone to GO who doesn't want to GO? I get it; we are all busy; we are all consumed with our own issues; it's hard to imagine finding extra time or to muster the desire to deal with other people and their problems. Time is a commodity and relationships can be very taxing, but we have to find God's heart for people and see our purpose in people.

There are many more ways in which people disqualify themselves, perhaps there are a few of your own, but still the command from Christ to us, His followers, is, GO! Make disciples. There are no caveats; there is no excuse too large to keep us from following Christ and His call to make disciples. In some way, somehow we have to find a passion for people, for His people and find a way to invest ourselves in making disciples. Don't be surprised to discover that passion often follows obedience. I am a big believer that God leads us to people and leads people to us, our family, friends, neighbors, coworkers, etc. We have to get in the game, ready and willing to allow our hearts to break for what breaks His, seeing those around us as those for whom Christ died.

COST

Easier said than done? Absolutely! There is no doubt that making disciples will challenge you, exhaust you and cost you. In discipleship you have to be there for people and that isn't easy, especially in this crazy busy 21st century. When we commit to make disciples, we are committing to people and that commitment cannot be taken lightly. Being a disciple, however, means making disciples. There is no room for casual followership. Jesus encountered many people of this ilk, who would casually follow Him, sometimes there were a great many. Perhaps they followed for some personal benefit, or curiosity, hoping to see some miracle, or get a free lunch. Whatever the reasons, Jesus wouldn't have it. On one particular occasion, He addressed this kind of casual follow-ship.

> *Now great multitudes went with Him. And He turned and said to them, "If anyone comes to Me and does not hate his father and mother, wife and children, brothers and sisters, yes, and his own life also, he cannot be My disciple. And whoever does not bear his cross and come*

*after Me cannot be My disciple. For which of you,
intending to build a tower, does not sit down first and
count the cost, whether he has enough to finish it— lest,
after he has laid the foundation, and is not able to finish,
all who see it begin to mock him, saying, 'This man began
to build and was not able to finish'? Or what king, going
to make war against another king, does not sit down first
and consider whether he is able with ten thousand to meet
him who comes against him with twenty thousand? Or
else, while the other is still a great way off, he sends a
delegation and asks conditions of peace. So likewise,
whoever of you does not forsake all that he has cannot be
My disciple.* (Luke 14:25-33)

If being a disciple means making disciples, then we have to
factor disciple-making into the cost. How will you budget
disciples into your life? Though the answer to this will look
different for everyone, one thing is common to all—a forsaking
of what you have. We forsake our time; we forsake our energy;
in some cases, we even forsake our money and resources to
make disciples. These are all vital Kingdom investments.

R.O.I.

One of the most basic concepts in investing is the R.O.I.,
Return On Investment. Investors will look over a potential
investment to see what the rate of return is before they deem it
worth the investment risk. This mindset looks at the trade off,
the yield, the result potential for investment of time, talent,
energy, and money. Jesus wants us to have this mindset for the
Kingdom; we are His heavenly investors building the Kingdom
of God one person at a time.

In Matthew 6: 19-21, Jesus says, "Do not lay up for
yourselves treasures on earth, where moth and rust destroy and
where thieves break in and steal; but lay up for yourselves

treasures in heaven, where neither moth nor rust destroys and where thieves do not break in and steal. For where your treasure is, there your heart will be also."

People work to get money, property, security, health, praise and a sense of accomplishment and worth. Most people want to make a difference in other people's lives. This has an intrinsic value, a boost to their sense of self to positively affect their community, and "oh let it be the world." This is the way God made us, the problem is, we often seek these rewards for the here and now and neglect both our own and others eternal rewards. Just so, one of the greatest investments you can make for your own spiritual health and for others good is to invest your life, your time, your energy and your money in making disciples who make disciples who make disciples. In any way you can. Do it any way you can. This rate of return has exponential growth potential for the Kingdom of God, not only in a spiritual tabulation, but for families and communities in the here and now.

I believe one of the hardest lessons for Jesus to get across was getting people to think with a Kingdom mindset, getting people's minds off of terra firma and onto spiritual not-so-firm-a was a constant frustration for Him. I've heard it said, "You don't want to be so heavenly minded that you're no earthly good," but, while I get the meaning, I don't think this is our real problem in the church. I don't know about you, but I have to work on not being so earthly minded that I'm no heavenly good. The Kingdom mindset is not a mere comprehension; it has to play out; it has to affect how we live, the decisions we make, the jobs we take and how we do them, the relationships we have and how we preserve them. It continually stretches our faith to constantly think eternally.

Right now, my wife and I are selling our house... again. We are lightening our load... again. Kingdom commitment is a constant vigilance to constantly entrench ourselves in comfort.

118

We are selling and moving again, so we can do more for the Kingdom. It is hard to leave the comforts we have built for ourselves here, to change routines, to downsize, to move to a new location, but we feel that we make a greater impact with our time, talents, relationships and resources in this phase of our ministry if we do. Right now, my wife and I believe that the greatest heavenly R.O.I. we can have is reaching as many people as possible, helping them engage in the Great Commission, making disciple-making disciples. This requires us to GO, to travel for a time, to reach, to teach, to encourage and inspire through our message and through our music. God has given us certain tools, and we want to invest them into building the Kingdom. It is exciting to believe that we can do more for Him, but there is a cost. There is always an earthly cost to count for a greater heavenly reward.

DO THE MATH

Let's say three people each make one disciple in the town I live, Longwood, Florida. These three each disciple three others in the same time it took my first mentors, Dave and Shelby, to prepare for discipling me—three months (I'm not suggesting that all the discipling is done, or that this is all the preparation time it takes, but it suits our scenario). In three months, these three new disciples take on their own disciple. This pattern continues doubling every three months. So, in three months, the first three become six; in three more months, the six become twelve; the twelve become 24; the 24 become 48... over and over, doubling every three months... you get the picture.

Given that there are about 14,000 people living in Longwood, how long would it take to disciple these 14,000 people? The answer... about three years. Impressive!

How long it would take to reach all of Florida's 20 million? The answer... about six years. Wow! Twice as long, only six years to disciple 20 million people!

Okay, what about the entire population of the planet, 7.4 billion people and counting? The answer... about eight years... doesn't make the "all the world" thing seem too crazy, or impossible. 8 years to disciple the whole world. That's mind blowing!

Perfect math is bound to breakdown in the face of stubborn hearts, but that's the power exponential growth that good disciple-making can have. I believe this is why Jesus spent three years with twelve guys and made them His number one priority. He understood the power of making disciples who make disciples, who make disciples, who make disciples... and so should we.

12

 GOALS & BOUNDARIES

1 Peter 2:2-3

As newborn babes, desire the pure milk of the word,
that you may grow thereby,
if indeed you have tasted that the Lord is gracious.

Jonathan:

In many ways, disciple-making is like parenting. Disciple-makers raise spiritual children. Like children, disciples go through stages of development—infancy, toddler, childhood, adolescence, adulthood.

The disciple needs the most care, nurturing and attention during their spiritual infancy and toddler stages. Here, they need to be fed, cleaned up, taught basics, but most of the emphasis should be on loving and encouraging them… and changing their diapers and potty-training them.

During the early and late childhood stages, there is more emphasis on learning, directing, watching and helping them develop independence. The long-range goal with raising a disciple, like a child, is always training them with the life skills, knowledge and wisdom needed to be productive, stable, and self-sustaining adults. They have to learn to make it on their own and how to raise up their own spiritual families.

So, in adulthood, the child is grown, independent and becoming parents themselves.

As every child learns and grows at their own pace, so does every disciple. People can crawl through these stages at a snail's pace, or soar through them with jet propulsion. There are a lot factors to the pacing of discipleship—intelligence, background, drive, education, temperament and personality, and even practiced self-control. The important thing to know is that it's individualized not programed.

I don't believe that a disciple needs to reach adulthood to take on a disciple of his or her own. David and Shelby, who disciple me originally, developed quickly, but were still probably more in an early childhood stage, at the time. They acted like a good older brother and sister, helping me to grow, feeding me, cleaning my face of "spit-up," etc. This brotherly, or sisterly approach to discipleship works best when there is parental/pastoral oversight, which there was.

This may help you in your approach to disciple-making. The amount of time, care, oversight and attention you give to a new disciple in the infancy stage ought to change, even lessen as they grow. I like to think about it as though we are raising people to be co-laborers. At some point, the discipleship relationship should balance out and level the field. This was Jesus' example. Jesus told His disciples, "No longer do I call you servants, for the servant does not know what his master is doing; but I have called you friends, for all that I have heard from my Father I have made known to you." (John 15:15)

GOALS

If I see someone who is willing and passionate to grow in Christ and feel that the Lord may be placing that someone on my heart, I invite them for some one-on-one time to investigate it further. If that goes well, I seek to initiate the personal discipleship process with something profound… like, "I'd like to disciple you." Subtle, right… well it's all in the art of the delivery. This kind of direct invitation sets the tone for our relationship. I want them to know that my primary intention is one of discipleship. I feel it's important get a commitment up front, so that we are both on the same page. It might feel weird to state it so baldly, as if you are being prideful, but the usual response I get from someone who is passionate to grow is extreme gratitude. Jesus said it just as baldly with His own disciples, saying, "Follow me and I will make you…." We figure He's a good role model for discipleship; His 12 changed the world, after all.

From that point, I like to set some clearly stated goals both for their spiritual development and for our discipleship relationship. As we've said many times in this book, my end goal with every discipleship relationship is to train up a new disciple-maker. I'm quite clear with this from the start.

Personal spiritual goals usually consist of a regular Bible study/devotional schedule, starting their prayer life and helping them to overcome sin and their own personal trials and temptations. This starts the accountability within the relationship. I invite them to call me whenever, and we work out a schedule to have one-on-one meetings, do counseling, if necessary (which it usually is since I tend to take on new believers), and get the disciple into my small group if he is not already a part of it.

I immediately begin looking for things that they can do to develop their leadership skills.

In small groups, as in the church, a direct approach of asking people and inviting people to serve works far better than waiting for people to volunteer. It is always good to have people work alongside of you, not for you. We have to be careful in our sending that we are not making them feel like our personal servants. If you are leading people, then here are some areas where you can get your disciples involved. You can have them take responsibility for things like opening and closing meetings in prayer, initiating questions and responses to the weekly discussions, praying for specific needs. You can have them share their testimony, publicly read scripture or small group materials. There are opportunities in the church as well, like ushering, taking up offerings, working on facility maintenance, getting them involved in the prayer team or some other programs. In services, when an appeal for salvation or some other altar call is given, it's a great idea to have people from the small groups enlisted and trained to pray with people and invite them to a small group. There are opportunities beyond all this as well; I look for changes to take them with me when I have special assignments like hospital visits, counseling, and evangelistic outreaches.

The SAVIOR Musical was the first thing I'd ever written as a Christian and our early performances were a discipleship extravaganza. The bassist, John Gunderson, was discipling me. Fil, who sang Peter, was a new believer that I'd been discipling. He never sang in his life, but he had a bit of a voice, so I threw him up there. The guitarist came to Christ at one of our first performances. The guy who ran video, the guy who ran sound, the guy who helped with booking, the people who helped with management, the people who printed our playbill books and lyrics, the people who helped set up and break down, and several other musicians and singers… were all new believers. The whole thing functioned as an evangelistic team and a discipleship group.

Here is the money. There is this wonderful spiritual blessing that you, as the disciple-maker, experience. Discipleship changes the discipler and not just the disciple. Remember the story of the woman at the well? Jesus speaks with her, she is blessed and runs off to tell her friends and family about Him. When Jesus' disciples come back from Subway with His lunch, Jesus refuses to eat, saying, "I have food to eat that you do not know about" (John 4:32). He was trying to tell them how fed and full He was by seeing the response of the woman He had just witnessed to—a life transformed. I get this. When you see someone overcome, grow, meet their spiritual goals, it feeds you, as the disciple-maker in some odd strange and spiritual way. It encourages you to go on, to become better yourself, to disciple more. When you see and experience this blessing, when you realize that He does use broken vessels to accomplish His work, you get a glimpse of the Father's heart and it is both amazing and humbling. This is the fruit of our labor.

Andrew:

I would have given my right arm to have someone make such an offer of discipleship and leadership development to me… one that entailed all that is discussed here. I wanted this so badly I got sucked into the Shepherding movement of the early to mid-80s, where the hope of leadership training turned into humiliating hoops to prove loyalty and complete submission. This group was so dysfunctional, so domineering and so drunk on the idea of shepherding power that I doubt you'd believe the stories I could tell. Like one shepherd, who boasted that he liked to call his disciples in the middle of the night to come over to his house to wash his dog or car, or another who demanded that his disciple refrain from marital relations unless he asked permission. One shepherd, [I swear I'm not lying.] was so into a "spiritual" discussion with the leaders of my church, that he peed into a cup and made his disciple carry it out for him so that he wouldn't have to leave the dialogue. This is just a smattering. I grew weary of this abuse quickly and headed out for other discipleship shores… which I only found once (for a single year) in the next 3 decades. Few have demonstrated genuine interest in me or offered this kind of growth opportunity in spite of my passion, stability, and intellectual capacity. For the most part, I had to carve out my own path and find my mentors in books.

I have set my heart, therefore, to become the discipler that I never had and to help future leaders find rewarding paths rather than clawing to reinvent the ministry wheel.

BOUNDARIES

Jonathan:

How do you know when it is *not* working? What is our response if the person we are discipling doesn't reciprocate like we'd hoped, or at all? What if he just refuses to wash your dog in the middle of the night? So, perhaps we need to discuss boundaries.

Yes, discipleship gets messy, complicated and often we don't know how or where to draw personal and spiritual lines. There are definitely people that will appreciate the time and attention you give them, they will grow from what you teach them and be encouraged knowing that you are there for them. There are also people who will not appreciate your time and the attention you give them, and even some who will take advantage of you. They say you should learn from other people's mistakes, hopefully you can glean from mine.

I met with a guy we will call Tommy. He was a young passionate guy in his early twenties. Having just come to Christ, he was pretty fired up for Jesus. He came out of a life of drug and alcohol abuse and had quit cold turkey. I saw his passion and witnessed his love for the Lord in our small group and also saw that, without discipleship, this passion could wane and the old habits and lifestyle kick back in. I felt I needed to get with him, so I had lunch with him and told him that I would like to disciple him. "Really!?" He was super excited which made me feel a little funny, *Man I'd better show up for this guy, he's really appreciative.* I gave him a book to use for his Bible study time and helped him in his prayer life. We talked about his personal struggles and set some small attainable goals. In the weeks that followed, he did great. We met for lunch regularly, he showed up to small group and to church services, he started influencing his friends at work and witnessing to them. Then, they started showing up to small group; about four of them came on a regular basis. They were great guys, and Tommy was helping them grow in Christ. They were even getting together outside of our group for impromptu Bible Studies. I was elated to see this kind of growth.

Then something happened. Tommy slipped up. He got high with one of his friends, and it really took a toll on him spiritually. We got him back in the group and spent more one-on-one time with him. Then he blew off a few one-on-ones with me, didn't show up for small group, wouldn't answer his phone. He fell back into his old habits. We got him to come back, the guys got around him, but he kept slipping up. No matter how many times we tried GOing to him, or getting him into a rehab program, something would happen to trip him up and hinder his walk with Christ.

This was beyond frustrating to witness. Eventually there came a point where I had to stop GOing to him. The discipleship relationship disintegrated when he stopped responding. I had to let him know that I would be there for him still if he ever wanted to talk, but I knew I had to let him go; I had to create a boundary. This had somewhat of a redemptive effect. Realizing the distance he'd created, he became motivated to come back. We loved him through his struggles even if it meant letting him go. We have to respect people's free will and their decisions, even if we don't agree with them. Thankfully, he's doing pretty good these days… at least according to the GPS tracker I put on his car. (Humor intended)

Discipleship boundary lines will differ for everyone, but we must have them, and must know where they are. The reason why we say this is because if you are badly burned once, you will be far less likely to risk GOing again. You have to have certain protections in place; you have to know what is and isn't a deal breaker; you have to know when to walk away and not be emotionally suckered into the black hole that can be other people's misery. The nature of these types of relationships can be not only time consuming, but spiritually exhausting and personally taxing. They can take a toll on our hearts and can even negatively affect other relationships in our lives.

There are many factors to consider in creating boundaries. We don't want to be aloof, and unapproachable, but we do need to balance our time and relationships wisely. There is a stewardship aspect that comes into play with boundary making. Resources like time, energy, and money are limited. We can't give in one area without taking away from another. Knowing where the balance lies between being there and giving too much, between supporting and enabling, between soft love and tough love is an act of discernment that develops over time with hard-won lessons.

I wanted to state this here, because I have often felt guilty, I didn't do enough for someone. I have been heartbroken seeing the choices some of my disciples have made. There will always be pain when we see people that we've invested in go down a bad path, but we have to create boundaries, even in our own hearts. I've been burned, let down, discouraged, frustrated, left feeling like a failure, but I had to create boundaries in my heart that drive home the reality that I can't do everything, that everyone is responsible for his or her own choices in life. If I couldn't see those lines, I'd be too discouraged to keep making disciples. I do what I can within reasonable boundaries, and leave people in God's hands, which is really where they've been the whole time. It hurts to let people go, but we work for the Lord and not every seed sown will fall on good soil and grow the way we'd most desire. We do our best to be good stewards, good sowers, good parents, there for them, loving them… and loving them means creating proper boundaries.

BURNT CHICKEN

I was working with a guy for about two or three years before my wife and I went on the road full time. Knowing our discipleship relationship would be strained by our travel, I invited him to rent a room from us in our house for a pittance. This would help in a few ways. He could watch the house while we were on the road, the partnership would keep us in constant contact, and we would, inevitably, catch up in the times that we were home. The little he paid in rent helped him to save money and help us with the bills. It was a win-win; he moved in.

He wasn't domestic. We'd come home to a dirty house, trash everywhere, the floors caked with food, smearing on everything including the TV screens. In three months, he scarcely mowed the lawn or took out the trash, and rats moved into my garage. His room smelled like a corpse… we almost checked to see if anyone was missing pets or children in the neighborhood. I won't even describe the bathroom.

He was reckless with our property. He melted our outdoor electric grill by filling it with coals and based on the black smoke stain on the side of the house, almost burned the place down. We found things randomly broken everywhere.

We returned from one long RV tour to a house that reeked of chemicals and charring; it's horror filled every inch of the place… it was so thick it could have been a solid; it made his bedroom smell like a field of wild roses in comparison. He told me that he had burned chicken on the cook-top by leaving it on the burner while he fell asleep in his room! Luckily the house didn't go up in flames.

Instead of calling in help, he tried to fix the situation himself and made matters worse. He put a chemical cleaner on the walls that bleach-stained the paint, used heavy chemicals in the ducts that made the air almost unbreathable, like a DOW plant; he bleached the stone counters and stripped them of their sealant. He confided to a mutual friend that he'd been drinking heavily the night he left the food cooking on the stove and had passed out in his room, waking to a house filled with smoke. I only found this out much later, however.

I kept calm with him and forgave him (meaning that I had

decided not to kill him) and asked only that he fix it. We couldn't stay inside, so my wife and I had to sleep in our RV in the driveway while we tried to get the stench out. No matter how much we cleaned, changed air filters, washed walls, counters, ceilings, we couldn't remove the smell. It was obvious that the situation needed professional attention, but since he'd done this, I wanted him to take control of the situation and set up the arrangements, handle the cleanup, make the calls to get an ozone machine in to remediate the damage. I gave him a detailed list of things that he needed to do. This was a mentoring move designed to redeem the situation and the relationship and to propel him into responsible adult living.

We were going to be gone for a week up to Nashville and told him to have the house repaired by the time we got back. He agreed, but when we returned home the place still stank. He did exactly what we told him NOT to do, and didn't do anything from the list. He redid all the chemical cleaning that had damaged everything and worsened the smell last time. This stressed our relationship with him, badly.

We finally had to take control and pay for a maid service, an ozone machine rental, air filters, counter cleaners, sealers, and paint. We had to repaint the inside of the house ourselves. It was quite a job, costing a good deal, but in the end, we got the smell out.

He agreed to pay us back for the damages, so we set up a payment plan that he didn't keep. This stressed out our relationship with him even more. He told me that in order to be able to afford to pay us back, he would have to move out. We wrote up another agreement and payment plan, but as soon as he moved out, what I feared would happen did—not only did he break his payment agreement with us, he cut off all communication.

After a few months, I was able to get a meeting with a mutual pastor who could mediate between us. I was shocked at the meeting to hear how unremorseful he was. I struggled with seeing how he could justify his actions, but somehow he could. I felt even more hurt by this, taken advantage of and sort of betrayed. I had a hard time with my emotions. I was downright angry, but I didn't want to feel like a victim, or fuel my anger by fixating on the injustice.

I wanted to restore the relationship, but how could things be restored? I even apologized in the meeting if I had said or done anything, been too stern with him during the ordeal, but none of this was reciprocated.

I had learned a valuable lesson in creating boundaries. Boundaries need to be established both relationally and in our hearts, knowing that people can and probably will hurt and disappoint us. Our job remains the same, however—make disciples as best as we can and trust God with our relationships.

13

 THE CONTENT OF DISCIPLESHIP:
A CALL TO TRAINING

MATTHEW 28:20

"...teaching them to observe all things that I have commanded you"

Andrew:

I attended a national three day conference on Discipleship several years back. The presenters had a long corresponding series of books on diverse aspects of their scheme for discipleship. The only thing missing from multiplied hours of discussion and even more books was content. At no point did anyone speak or write about what a disciple should learn or what a mentor should train into a disciple other than the processes of the discipleship model they were using.

In a revitalization seminar I attended, the speaker used Mark Dever's *Nine Marks of a Healthy Church* as his own paradigm, but contemptuously dismissed any need to discuss four of his content-based marks with the wave of a hand, sneering, "I think we can assume solid teaching." I thought, *We can ASSUME the most essential part of the paradigm? A revitalization seminar speaker feels that he has no need to bother with the most essential revitalizing force of Christianity?* Indeed, he was certain that his methodology without the message was sufficient, as if the real secret to transformative discipleship is found in organization rather than in a powerful encounter with Jesus Christ and His

Word? Sad as it may seem, I encounter this attitude everywhere I GO.

Method and organization are important, but the truth is, if we build on anything other than the teachings of Christianity, the worldview of Christianity, the standards of Christianity, the book of Christianity, the Gospel of Christianity, The Christ of Christianity then all we have is a business strategy with a highly personal component. Cults have been doing this for ages. *Welcome, check your coat and brains at the door, grab a Dixie cup of Kool-Aid and have a seat.*

Jesus said, "GO therefore and make disciples of all the nations, baptizing them in the name of the Father and of the Son and of the Holy Spirit, teaching them to observe all things that I have commanded you." This chapter is about the "teaching them to…" part. I want to discuss what "observe all things that I have commanded you" looks like in a modern context. This involves both knowing and doing… or not doing, as the case may be. Indeed, a vast portion of discipleship in the early years may be taken up with teaching people to be decent, self-controlled, self-sacrificing and moral human beings. We've discussed behavior modification through discipleship a bit already. So, most of what remains to be discussed is the knowing part… it bolsters the doing part. Disciples may, like a children, start by doing without understanding, but they won't, like adults, continue doing unless understanding comes.

MAKING LEADERS

When we say, *make disciples*, we mean, *make disciple-making disciples*, which translates into, *train leaders*. We recognize that not everyone will be fit or qualified for leadership at any given level, but any disciple-making scheme must have replicating leadership as a primary focus. Leadership training focuses on character, process, practice and, yes… education.

I learned a lot about essential teachings in a discipleship setting while building a bible college in Pune, India. Developing leadership training programs for village students proved a unique challenge. As westerners, we took for granted the vast amount of basic knowledge that even the worst American public schools provide… a world of knowledge that good leaders need. In India, we could not even pretend that such knowledge was other people's responsibility. Everything that our future leaders needed to know, or needed to know how to do, in order to be good leaders, became our responsibility.

Our team's first great challenge was defining the word "need," as in, everything they "need" to know to be good leaders. Two mentalities vied for control.

Those with a minimalist mentality believed that students who were only going to be village pastors didn't need to know much. How hard is it to have services once or twice a week? A little message from the Bible, some singing, taking up an offering, doing the occasional baptism, wedding or funeral… no big deal.

Those with the maximalist mentality wanted to train leaders for the future of an increasingly globalized India, not merely "village pastors." We wanted to equip every student to their maximum potential, so that our leaders could compete with the most educated among the Hindus and Muslims and Buddhists, and help all their people to build a thriving and transformative church AND stable community.

I can sum up the challenge in a single confrontation with a nearby Bible college president in India. During a visit, when he discovered my intentions to explain a passage of scripture in the next morning's service, he angrily said, "We don't teach our people the Bible; we simply tell them what they must do." Let me paraphrase. *We don't create self-sustaining disciples; we make intellectual and emotional slaves. We don't introduce our people to the Savior to learn at his Scriptural feet; we make ourselves indispensable gateways to Him. We don't raise up future leaders; we create spiritually crippled dependents. We don't train thinking servants of Christ; we train mimics of ourselves and parrots to replicate our programs.*

This minimalist mindset is not an India problem; it is a human problem; it is a Church problem. It's a problem that can, most definitely, affect our approach to discipleship. It limits the mentor in what he or she deems worth teaching, and it limits the disciple in what he or she deems worth expending the energy to learn.

You may have heard of the dumbing down of America; I believe that we are witnessing the dumbing down of the Church, and the great enabler of this epidemic ignorance is the minimalist mindset of leaders and congregants alike.

The minimalist mindset is shortsighted. It concerns itself with expediency, immediate knowledge to meet immediate demands, rather than growth through a transformation of processes.

Minimalism seeks to preserve a leader's sense of control. The last thing the minimalist mind wants is to allow people the autonomy to explore, to develop, to re-invent. Knowledge is power, and the minimalist doesn't share power. *Does the farmer explain the big plan to the mule pulling his plow? Does the master chef share the secret recipe with the wait staff? Does the owner tell his business to his dock workers? If you give a man a fish, you feed him for a day, but if you teach a man to fish, he no longer needs you to get fish... so, whatever you do, don't teach a man to fish.*

The minimalist minded leader views others as tools for advancing the status quo. Resources are limited and time and energy should not be wasted on things that do not *appear* relevant to performing daily tasks. *Why waste time teaching a woman to read when her job is to manage the pressing domestic affairs of those who are working the fields or hunting down meat? Why should a man learn about art when his job is to tend animals and crops? Who cares if small group leaders know church history when all we need then to do is facilitate the discussion around the packaged material purchased for that group? Why should worship leaders study theology when all we need them to do is lead the congregation in song? Why should pastors bother with Greek, Hebrew and Aramiac when their most essential duties involve administration, visionary direction, and popping out a hundred or so 20 minute talks a year… don't we have translations, commentaries, and Google to cover all that?*

When I started looking at the arrival state of our students from villages that didn't even have electricity or plumbing, I was forced to contemplate the distance between them and true leadership qualification. Not that one needs electricity to be a leader… otherwise even Jesus would be out. But they emerged from subsistence farming communities and, more often than not, had little to no knowledge of anything outside of the barest information needed to survive in those environments.

We had to ask ourselves whether we were content to minimally equip them to govern a mud hut village church in the most basic rudiments of the Christian faith (come to school, memorize our lessons, go home and teach them verbatim until you die) or whether we wanted to train them as best we could to be life-learning, creative, problem-solving, academically astute, spiritual leaders and visionaries. If the former, almost any indoctrination in orthodox positions would do. If the latter, we needed to establish a guiding star vision for what that type of leadership training entailed and the steps needed to maximize our efforts on our student's behalf with the time and resources we had available to us.

GUIDING STAR VISION

I'd like to share that guiding star vision with you and discuss some practical steps in raising up disciples that march steadily toward that star throughout their lives. This is not a quick fix, nor a one-size-fits-all offering. It contains many things that most Christians would consider too "worldly" for church.

As with any vision, its attainment starts with big-picture pieces and grows more detailed and specialized as it goes; both distance and speed should depend on the interest, commitment and capacity of each disciple, not on our dismissal or limitation of the vision. It is also dependent on one's ability to recognize his or her limitations as a mentor and to have a willingness as leaders to not only allow, but to assist disciples in moving on to other mentors more qualified to guide them in certain areas.

Let's begin with a handful of essential qualities and stages that, while often too "unspiritual" for church and Christian discipleship, are essential to training qualified leaders.

The Greeks had a great way of organizing their thoughts about education. They sought to move a student through three stages of learning: Grammar, Logic, and Rhetoric.

The Grammar stage represents a mass exposure to raw data, facts upon facts about science, math, the world, society, history, literature, etc... This provides the student with the materials necessary for building real knowledge. Never confuse a person's ability to look something up on Google for real knowledge. Knowledge is not access to facts; knowledge is in absorbing and storing facts and in knowing what to do with those accumulated facts.

The student who is given many facts is slowly drawn into **the Logic stage**, which involves learning logical relationships and processes and the art of connecting data into paradigms used to explain and order life and to solve problems. This is critical thinking, making basic judgments about the world in light of all the stuff a person knows.

In **the Rhetorical stage,** the student learns through trial and error to question existing paradigms critically, to postulate new theories, and to develop persuasive methods for testing and presenting them.

Thus, the building blocks of raising up properly equipped leaders, while "unspiritual," are the development of skills of Memorization, Critical Thinking, and Creative Thinking.

These require learning agility, mental and emotional adaptability and flexibility, and the social capacity for both teamwork and a healthy contesting of ideas, meaning that you know how to dialogue and disagree without pitching a fit or shutting down.

This brings us to my deepest passion—actual content. If we memorize, think critically and creatively, we have to memorize, criticize and be creative with something.

What is that something?

I run a double risk by detailing my long range vision for leadership training.

If you are a minister being asked to disciple disciple-making disciples, my guiding star vision can end up feeling more like an overwhelming burden that cripples you with discouragement before you are even out of the discipleship starting gate. *How am I supposed to do all that and run a church of X number of people? Isn't that what Bible college and seminary is for? I don't even have a full grasp on that stuff, how am I supposed to teach it to others?*

To this I warn, don't take the burden fully on yourself; learn to utilize the resources available to you, especially when those resources are other people gifted in areas you are not. Get a vision for training leaders and become part of, not the whole of, that process. Don't limit your disciples to what you are personally able to give them. This requires humility.

As for your own standing in the vision, be a life-learner. Be constantly and intentionally seeking opportunities to develop yourself in all the areas discussed below. Audit courses. Read books. Read journal articles. Follow blogs. Look for opportunities to redeem wasted time for learning. Personally, I listen to recorded books and university courses while I drive. In the last 15 years, I've literally taken in over a thousand books and more than 30 university courses on everything from philosophy, history, biblical studies, linguistics, economics, psychology, specialized science subjects, and writing and literature. I drive a lot.

If you are a would-be leader interested in getting more involved in disciple-making, my guiding star vision might easily overwhelm your mind and make you feel like you have nothing to offer until you've mastered a good portion of it, or cause a kick back in favor of more mystical criteria for leadership. *I was a terrible student in school, how am I supposed to learn all this stuff? Who's got time to learn all this? If this is what it takes, I'll never know enough to be qualified to lead. What does all this have to do with being a church leader, shouldn't I just learn to hear from God?*

Let me encourage you. A guiding star vision is something grand that keeps you moving in a certain direction FOREVER; it is not a starting point and it's never an ending point.

When I was a young teenager, I was chatting on the phone with a young lady who had captured my fancy, and my little brother picked up the other line, screaming, "The dryer is on fire!!!!" I rushed into the basement and, sure enough, flames were shooting out of the door. As I yanked the dryer door open and started pulling out burning clothes to stamp them out on the cement floor, I order him, "Get me water!" He came back way too fast with a tiny juice glass and held it out to me as I continued stamping. I looked up and snarled, "Is that really the best you could do?" He looked down at what he had offered me, as if for the first time, blushed with embarrassment and ran away with his tiny offering to get something more substantive. Later, after the fire was out, I said to him, "David, the juice glass wasn't much, but the least you could have done is thrown it on the fire before you left." Don't let the realization of how much there is to know keep you from continuing to learn it. Bring what you have. Throw it on the fire. Then go get a little bigger helping and throw that on the fire too.

With that, let me say that leadership training worthy of the name should, through a variety of venues (i.e. church, bible studies, classes, small groups, mentorship, etc), draw disciples into:

1. Global literacy

2. Cultural literacy

3. Biblical literacy,

4. Christian literacy, and

5. Ministry Mentorship

I love the term **literacy.** I adopted it as my own from the educational visionary E. D. Hirsch. I use it to describe a person who is functional in a particular environment by having the essential knowledge needed to survive and thrive in it. I am, for instance, highly literate in areas of Bible and Theology, but less so in financial markets, and even less so in molecular biology. Okay, I'm illiterate in molecular biology.

Global Literacy means being aware of the big bad world around you. Future leaders should, over time, gain at least a rudimentary knowledge of those subjects generally included under the rubric, Liberal Arts education—Science, Arts, Literature, History, Economics, etc. While these may seem off topic for the training of Christian leaders, for a person to be a Christian leader, he or she must be a leader, and leaders ought to be well-rounded and have a big picture of reality and possibility. It's a complicated world and pat and unexamined answers won't do. Therefore, the general broadening of the mind is rarely a waste of time or resources. Christian leaders are meant to equip disciples for the work of the ministry, making them ready laborers in God's diverse harvest. General learning enriches the soul and empowers a person to give a meaningful defense of the faith in this complex and hostile world.

Cultural Literacy means:

1. Knowing what culture is and how to discern it.

2. Knowing how essential culture is for understanding and engaging any person.

3. Knowing that you have a culture, and being able to fully engage it.

4. Knowing that your culture is only one among many.

5. Knowing that every culture has its pros and cons, failures and successes, consequences and rewards… including your own.

6. Knowing how to engage and evaluate other cultures meaningfully, developing cross-cultural communication skills.

It's a big world, and we've been called to reach it and make disciples from one end of it to the other. Disciple-making is communication and communication demands the ability to speak and listen articulately in every context in which we find ourselves. Without cultural literacy, we are severely hindered in our ability to GO into all the world, making disciples and teaching them to obey all that Christ has commanded. Without it, we easily confuse our culture and its values with biblical Christianity, and end up being preachers of culture rather than gospel.

Biblical Literacy means that a person is reasonably functional in interpreting and applying the Scriptures. This means being able to properly observe the Scriptures, being able to ask the right kinds of penetrating questions, being able to go to the right sources for getting proper answers to those questions, and being able to make effective use of those answers in life and ministry. Biblical Literacy should be the primary competency that mentors strive to provide disciples as they reorient their worldview, allowing sacred text, properly understood and applied, to challenge the most basic assumptions that they have about God, man and reality. Everything else that a minister does should flow from here in his or her theology, evangelism, preaching, disciplining, apologetics, church planting and general church leading and developing. And, by the way, *Global Literacy* provides the mental wherewithal to engage scripture intelligently, and *Cultural Literacy* allows a reader to engage the intentions of the inspired biblical authors in context.

A word to the wise: If you intend on being full-time in Christian ministry, do yourself a favor and learn biblical languages. If done well, with an eye to interpretation and effective use of scholarly resources, a journey of wondrous discovery awaits you… and it's easier than you think with a good teacher.

Christian Literacy means learning to see one's self as a connected part of the Christian Church whose history is almost 2000 years old, whose roots are buried in the soil of Ancient YHWHism and Judaism, and whose branches extend into a host of nations, cultures, and languages. To be Christian is to be part of an ancient and global community of the Old and New Testaments, a community that has been developing and changing to confront the ageless chaos that is human nature in ever-shifting, constantly morphing cultural expression. Our first allegiance, of course, is to God and Christ as revealed in sacred text, and we should not be completely hemmed in by the church's flawed historical or traditional comprehensions of those texts, nevertheless, to be Christian means that one stands in community with this history and those traditions and answers to them for choices made in the present. One can only drift so far before he or she is no longer rightfully part of what has traditionally been called Christianity.

As for **Ministry Mentorship**, there are certain things that can only be learned well by doing them. Exposure to different theories and philosophies about practical ministry has a measure of value, people's imaginations often need help when it comes to process improvement, after all, but only the practice of certain disciplines can bring true understanding and skill. For these, only mentorship will do. Jesus was intentional about leadership training. He had His three. He had His 12. He had His seventy. He had his followers. He did, they watched. They did, He watched. He sent them, they did, He debriefed. They got in trouble, He stepped in to shore up. He left, they continued on… He sent them the help of the Holy Spirit.

NEXT STEPS

I started by saying that I wanted to discuss what "observe all things that I have commanded you" looks like in a modern context. In a modern context, post-2000 years of Christian practice, theology and scholarship, there is a lot more involved in observing all things that Christ commanded than even Jesus' own disciples faced. These commands from Christ (like *be people of the book*) come to us across time, space, and culture and meet us in a world shaped by these commands in surprising ways. Our engagement of Jesus' commands is entangled by millennia of tradition and multiplied centuries of rich and meaningful contemplation by long dead brothers and sisters in Christ. We also need to transmit these commands into a modern, global, culturally diverse world that has been shaped by specific historical realities, political endeavors, and both scientific and technological wonders. *Global Literacy, Cultural Literacy, Biblical Literacy* and *Christian Literacy* are vital components to becoming increasingly effective 21st century disciple-making disciples.

A few practical steps:

To the Congregant:

- Make becoming a leader a priority.
- Take stock of your present educational level in the five areas I've discussed. Don't be embarrassed, just be honest, and make filling in gaps in that education a priority. Even after I finished my PhD in Theology, I did this, and concluded that I had several holes in my general education background. Here are some steps I took.
  - o I purchased textbooks and one by one kept them in the bathroom (TMI, I know) but in six years of doing this, I used that time to read through about 10 of them… Yes! Ten course text books on philosophy, economics, and political theory all while redeeming normally wasted time.
  - o I have purchased specific courses from "The Great Courses" and listen to them while I drive, as I've already noted. I also use my drive time to listen to recorded books. The last 15 years would have passed with or without doing this, but with it, I've taken in over a thousand books and some 30 university courses in addition to my official educational degree programs.
- There is a wealth of information available online. Seek out someone who specializes in the area of interest and get advice on how to discern the good from the bad.

To the pastor

- If you have a large church, you could run a serious educational program in it for training leaders in these areas, hiring ministers on staff whose time and energy are primarily dedicated to training leaders and whose own education and talents have equipped them to cultivate this type of learning. (I am currently on staff at a church of 500, and have been hired as an academic to build just such a program.)

• If you have a small church, you could develop a relationship with a local Bible School, Christian College, or Seminary that can give you access to this type of training for potential leaders in your congregation. Consider getting involved with, or recommend the launch of, co-operative mentorship programs for burgeoning leaders at such places.

• There is also a rich availability of more serious educational materials on line and through correspondence programs like Gordon-Conwell's Semlink, and The Assembly of God's Global University.

• Regardless of the size of your church, consider building a church library replete with the resources needed for meaningful engagement of cultural, Biblical and Christian literacy.

• Make the mentoring of leaders a priority, and take advantage of various educational opportunities (like special seminars, Sunday school, and alternate plans for different types of services…) in order to provide needed but often overlooked learning. One pastor Friend of mine did exegetical preaching on Sunday mornings, topical studies on Sunday nights, and book studies on Wednesday nights, and used Sunday School to introduce alternate educational interests, like Church History, Systematic Theology.

14

 STARTING SOMEWHERE

Matthew 28:18-20

Jesus came and spoke to them, saying, "All authority has been given to Me in heaven and on earth. Go therefore and make disciples of all the nations, baptizing them in the name of the Father and of the Son and of the Holy Spirit, teaching them to observe all things that I have commanded you; and lo, I am with you always, even to the end of the age." Amen.

Jonathan:

It's fun to coast down a big hill on a sled or a bike… just take your feet off the pedals and *weeeeeee!!!!* Coasting in life, however, can have quite negative effects. This is because life is a constant struggle against the forces of chaos. If we are not careful, we can easily find ourselves coasting backwards into social and spiritual ruin. Living a quality spiritual life is like walking up a down escalator. If you stand still, you're going backwards. If we are not gaining, we're losing.

I drive our RV all over the country, and I love to set the cruise control on a long stretch of highway. I get to kick off my shoes and relax my feet… get up, go in the back and get a drink… well, no! Cruise control isn't autopilot in either RV's or life. We often need rest in our spiritual lives, Sabbaths where we can recharge, cruise, but, at some point we have to get GOing again. In order to make disciples, we have to shut off our spiritual cruise control. We have to intentionally navigate the course and step on the gas. We have to find somewhere to start, or reengage with this mission of disciple-making.

GETTING GOing!

Airplanes face the greatest resistance of inertia getting off the runway. Getting started in making disciples can be no different. we will face resistance, but we must push ourselves to start somewhere with someone, somehow. If you've got something GOing, great! Keep GOing. Hopefully this book has helped you gain some ideas to keep momentum and focus direction. Here, I would like to give some practical starters, things we can do to either get started, or improve upon our development of making disciple-makers. Jesus said, "Ask, and it will be given to you; seek, and you will find; knock, and it will be opened to you" (Matthew 7:7). This is a good way to keep these starter steps in mind:

- *Ask* the Lord to place people on your heart whom you can disciple
- *Seek* them out. Keep on the lookout, be alert and pay attention to the relationships in your life, your friends, your family, people in your church, your workplace, etc.
- *Knock* on the doors, reach out to people, invite them out one-on-one, get the personal discipleship started.

STARTING SMALL GROUPS

Perhaps you picked up this book, or have been motivated through the reading to start a discipleship based small group ministry at your church. Here are some helpful steps to get you started.

- *Start with the goal in mind.* Discipleship based small groups are designed to make disciple-making disciples. That is their goal, how they function and their sole purpose.
- *Have a vision.* Have a clear idea of what this could look like

in your church and in your community.

- *Train your leaders.* Though not a hard and fast rule for me, it's advisable that you start with mature believers whom you trust, and who are passionate to make disciples. Training can cover points made in this book (Ch. 7 & 8 especially) on how to run a group:
  - ○ Keep the groups conversational
  - ○ Ask questions
  - ○ Be sensitive to the Holy Spirit during the group
  - ○ Meet in predictable, safe environments
  - ○ Develop a culture of safety
  - ○ Create a social covenant with the group members (Ch. 7)
  - ○ Work from good curriculum. It's advisable to start out with something gospel centric with good questions… we recommend *40 Days With the SAVIOR*… but, then, we're partial.
  - ○ Keep the small group small
  - ○ Look out for future leaders
  - ○ Raise other leaders from the groups, teaching the importance of one-on-ones and commitment to the personal discipleship process.
- *Invite the church.* If you're starting small, you want to do this incrementally, if not, invite them all.
- *It comes from the head.* Get the buy in from the lead pastor. If that's you, convince yourself. It has been our experience that one of the biggest reasons why small groups do not rise to their greatest potential within the church is because of a lack of buy-in and involvement by the lead pastor. Rather than falling into another church program, if the pastor talks about the importance of small groups, teaches on personal discipleship and promotes small groups, then there is a greater chance of success for the overall church.

GO THEREFORE!

Jesus said, "All authority has been given to Me in heaven and on earth. Go therefore and make disciples of all the nations" (Matthew 28:18) I've heard it said that when you see a "therefore" in the Bible, you should ask *what-is-it-there-for?* A little corny, I know, but, in this case, it's a great question.

Jesus said that He has been given ALL... not some, not part, not even a lot... but, ALL *authority*, GO therefore. He not only authorizes you and I to GO, but this kind of "all authority" comes with "all power." It's like He's saying to His Disciples and to you and I, "Hey listen, I've have power over everything, *authority* over everything; there is nothing too great for Me; I want you to make disciples. I've got you; just GO! He's got your back. He will empower you and equip you. He will open doors for you. He will lead you and show you the how's and who's. He gives you His Spirit, His Wisdom, His creativity... therefore, GO! GO! GO!

61521766R10089

Made in the USA
Charleston, SC
21 September 2016